500
BEAUTIFUL
WORDS
YOU SHOULD
KNOW

Also by Caroline Taggart

500 Words You Should Know

Improve Your Word Power

500 BEAUTIFUL WORDS YOU SHOULD KNOW

CAROLINE TAGGART

Michael O'Mara Books Limited

First published in Great Britain in 2020 by

Michael O'Mara Books Limited
9 Lion Yard
Tremadoc Road
London SW4 7NQ

A CIP catalogue record for this book is available from the British
Library.

Papers used by Michael O'Mara Books Limited are natural,
recyclable products made from wood grown in sustainable
forests. The manufacturing processes conform to the
environmental regulations of the country of origin.

ISBN: 978-1-78929-227-5 in hardback print format
ISBN: 978-1-78929-228-2 in ebook format

1 2 3 4 5 6 7 8 9 10

Designed and typeset by K.DESIGN, Winscombe, Somerset
Printed and bound by CPI Group (UK) Ltd, Croydon, CR0 4YY

www.mombooks.com

MIX
Paper from
responsible sources
FSC
www.fsc.org   FSC® C020471

Contents

Introduction

The first question that arises, of course, is 'What makes a beautiful word?' Or, if you prefer, 'What makes a word beautiful?' Any answer to either question is going to be subjective.

A few years ago, I wrote a book called *500 Words You Should Know* and said in its introduction that I had chosen the words entirely on the basis of having thought, 'Ooh, that's a nice word.' With 'beautiful' words I have tried to be a bit more specific. Yes, there are plenty that trip off the tongue beautifully – AMBROSIA, CELESTIAL, MELLIFLUOUS – and many more that satisfy the desire we all occasionally feel to sound clever – ASSEVERATE, CYNOSURE, RECIDIVIST. But the *Oxford English Dictionary* (*OED*) gives a secondary definition of 'beautiful' – not pleasing to the sight or other physical senses, but 'pleasing to the mind, especially in being appropriate or well suited to a particular purpose'. This gives me the opportunity to include words that are especially apt for their function, that mean what they sound as if they ought to mean and are pleasing as a result. In 1880, Sir James Murray, the first editor of the *OED*, coined the term 'echoic' for this sort of thing: his dictionary uses it 'to describe formations that echo the sound which they are intended to denote or symbolize'. Examples that I have included are FLIBBERTIGIBBET, GUFFAW, TWADDLE and – perhaps extending the *OED*'s definition a little to suit my own purposes – ADAMANT, DOLLOP and FILIGREE.

Moving on, you will find words for when you need to let off steam or to tell someone who has annoyed you what you think of them, such as APOPLECTIC, CATACLYSM and, one of my real favourites, FUSTIAN. Again, these may not be beautiful in the most conventional sense of the word, but goodness they make you feel better.

Shorter chapters encompass words that make you laugh, or at least smile, when you say them, of which perhaps the greatest is BORBORYGMUS, the noise produced by a rumbling gut; and words for things you didn't know there was a word for, in which you will go a long way to beat CHARIVARI, a discordant mock serenade made to newlyweds.

But when all is said and done, beauty is in the eye (or, perhaps in this context, the ear) of the beholder. I've chosen these words because I like them – and I hope you will too.

Caroline Taggart
September 2020

CHAPTER ONE

Words That Are Perfect for Their Meaning

A 'beautiful' word doesn't have to be long and flowing; sometimes it just has to be fit for purpose. The English language is blessed with lots of short, sharp words representing short, sharp actions, soft-sounding words for soft things and others that simply feel right. Here are a few.

accost

To go up and speak to someone, normally in a public place: 'A woman *accosted* me in the street and asked me to sample a new brand of yoghurt.' From an Old French word with various meanings to do with nearness, especially of a ship travelling close to the *coast*.

adamant

A hard-sounding word for a hard concept: if you're *adamant* about something you are convinced that it is true and you're not going to change your mind at any price. It derives from the name of an otherwise unidentified rock or mineral, sometimes confused with a diamond, and legendary for its hardness and impenetrability; both can probably trace their origins back to the Greek for 'unconquerable'.

amalgam

A mixture or blend, originally a combination of mercury and another metal, formerly used in dental fillings. Now it can be a mixture of almost anything: 'His character was an *amalgam* of patience and good humour.' The verb *to amalgamate* is often used to designate the merging of two or more businesses and the result is not an *amalgam* but an *amalgamation*.

amorphous

Anything with *morph* in it is likely to be about shape,
as in Franz Kafka's 1915 novella *The Metamorphosis*, in
which the protagonist wakes up to find he has changed
into an enormous insect; or in the sort of film where
an unassuming personage *morphs* into a superhero.
Amorphous, therefore, means lacking in a clearly defined
shape, having no particular style or characteristics: 'I
was trying to paint a cloudy sky, but it came out as an
amorphous grey blob.'

askance

To view someone or something *askance* is literally to
look at them at an angle, from an OBLIQUE perspective,
but it's normally used in the metaphorical sense of to be
disapproving, to distrust them: 'The board looked *askance*
at the new CEO's plans for restructuring.' Of uncertain
origin, but perhaps ultimately from the Latin for 'as if' and
therefore loosely related to QUASI.

bagatelle

A pretty word for a pretty little thing: something
decorative but of minimal significance – very often used
in the expression *a mere bagatelle*. The name can also be
applied to a short piece of piano music, the most famous
being that staple of children's piano lessons, Beethoven's
Für Elise. And there is a game called bagatelle which
takes various forms – it can be a sort of bar billiards, or
something played on a board with a spring-like handle,
a miniature pinball machine. *Bagatelle* comes from an

Italian term for 'a little property' (related to *bag* and *baggage*), but the game takes its name from the Château de Bagatelle, a pleasure garden on the fringes of Paris, where the bar-billiards version was first played in the time of Louis XVI and Marie Antoinette.

bedraggled

There's an infrequently used word *draggle*, which means to *drag* something through water or mud; as a result, it becomes *bedraggled*. It's the way you look when you've just come in out of the rain: your clothes are wet and dirty, and your hair is hanging limply around your ears. You'll probably want a towel for the dog, too.

blitz

The German for 'lightning', this entered English usage during the Second World War as an abbreviation of *blitzkrieg*, 'lightning war', the term used for the campaign of concentrated bombing attacks on British cities in 1940 and 1941. *The Blitz,* with a capital B, refers to that period, but in all lower case it has come to mean a less murderous form of hectic activity: you can have *a blitz on the housework*, for example, or *a blitz on the filing* – a short, focused assault on something you've probably been neglecting for a while. See also FLAK.

brook

Not the babbling kind, but the verb that means to tolerate, to put up with. It originally meant to enjoy the use of, to benefit from and was often found in legal contexts; nowadays it is generally used with a negative in expressions such as 'He will *brook* no delay – he says it's urgent' or 'He will *brook* no opposition – we've got to do it his way.' There's a mock-heroic tone to this word, so it's probably best not to use it unless you intend to be slightly sarcastic.

brunt

A short, sharp blow or sudden attack, or the impact of it. Often used in a figurative sense: 'I had borne the *brunt* of his bad temper for years.' Of unknown origin, though it's tempting to fantasize that it's a combination of a *blow* and the resulting *grunt*.

cacophony

A loud or unpleasant noise, particularly a discordant mixture of badly tuned instruments, or voices at a meeting where tempers are fraying. *Caco-* comes from the Greek for 'bad' and gives us a number of other unpleasant concepts – including a *cacotopia*, a place where everything is as bad as it can possibly be, even worse than a *dystopia*; and *cacology*, a bad choice of words or poor pronunciation. See also KAKISTOCRACY.

capacious

Roomy, full of *capacity* and therefore able to carry lots of
things. In Oscar Wilde's 1895 play *The Importance of Being
Earnest*, Miss Prism describes her famous handbag as 'old,
but capacious': in what she refers to as a moment of mental
abstraction, she was able to put a baby into it, so it must
have been *capacious* indeed.

caper

As a verb, to dance or prance about, to behave playfully; as
a noun, a movement of that kind or a prank, an escapade:
'He should have been home hours ago, so he must be up
to some *caper* or other.' It can trace its origins back to the
Latin for 'a goat' (as in the zodiac sign *Capricorn*); nothing
to do with the *caper* you might find on a pizza, which is the
flower bud of a Mediterranean shrub whose name is Greek
in origin.

cherish

To hold dear and to care for accordingly, to treasure. In
traditional versions of the Christian marriage service, the
partners promise to *love and cherish* each other, but you
can also *cherish* an idea: 'He *cherished* the hope that one
day he would be able to visit Antarctica.' Related to the
French *cher/chère* and *chéri(e)*, meaning 'dear'.

craw

Literally the crop of a bird, the pouch at the top of the digestive tract where food is stored and digestion begins. So, if a human says that something *stuck in their craw*, it means they couldn't stomach it, really resented it: 'It sticks in my *craw* that she should have got such good marks, when she didn't do nearly as much work as I did.'

crestfallen

If a rooster's *crest* – his crowning glory – were to *fall* or droop, he would look *crestfallen*: woebegone, disappointed, dejected. The word can be used of people, too, whether or not they have crests: 'He was *crestfallen* when the rally was cancelled: he'd been looking forward to it all year.' It's possible also to be *chap-fallen* or *chop-fallen* when your *chaps* or *chops,* on either side of your jaw, droop – again with disappointment or misery.

defunct

Dead, no longer in existence, no longer *functioning*. It was formerly used of a deceased person in the way we now usually use *late*, such as *the defunct duke, uncle of the present one.* Nowadays it's more often applied to institutions, periodicals and the like: *the defunct Social Democratic Party* or *the defunct* Today *newspaper.*

despondent

Lacking in hope – not quite despairing, but discouraged and dispirited. Lord Chesterfield, the eighteenth-century aristocrat known for his instructive letters to his son, advised against this feeling: 'Aim at perfection ... they who aim at it, and persevere, will come much nearer [to] it than those whose laziness and *despondency* make them give it up as unattainable.'

diffident

Shy, lacking faith in yourself – from the same Latin root as *fidelity* and *confident*. You might be *a diffident person*, have *a diffident nature* or make *a diffident remark* if you didn't think anyone wanted to hear what you had to say.

doldrums

An area close to the equator where north-east and south-east trade winds converge, making the winds in the region light and unpredictable. In the days when ships relied on wind power, they were often becalmed here. Metaphorically, therefore, being *in the doldrums* came to mean down in the dumps, in low spirits; it could also be used of a project that had ceased to make progress: 'We've spent the current budget, so we're in the *doldrums* until the new financial year.' Of uncertain origin, possibly based on an old word for dull or stupid.

dollop

Originally a clump of weeds or a patch of grass, this now means a large and shapeless quantity of anything – often a spoonful (or more) of cream or ice cream. It needn't be pleasant, though, and it needn't be a physical thing: you could answer a silly question with *a dollop of sarcasm*. See GLOOP for a similar concept.

doughty

Hardy, brave, determined. A slightly old-fashioned word: *a doughty steed* would once have carried you into battle without complaint and perhaps enabled you to perform *doughty deeds*. Today, an activist might wage *a doughty campaign* for their cause, while a long-distance runner might put in *a doughty performance.* It's from an old Germanic word for 'excellence' or 'strength', and is pronounced as if it were spelled 'doubty'.

dragoon

As a noun, this means a sort of mounted soldier (one who historically carried a 'fire-breathing' musket that resembled a *dragon*). When it was later used as a verb, it first meant *to set dragoons upon*, and thus became 'to coerce', to force someone to do something against their will: 'He was *dragooned* into helping to organize the concert.'

embezzle

To take someone else's money to use yourself, specifically when you are in a position of authority or trust and should be looking after that money. A burglar doesn't *embezzle* your savings, but a dishonest bank manager might. From an Anglo-Norman word meaning 'to make away with'. See also MISAPPROPRIATE.

felicity

A posh, Latin-derived word for 'happiness'. If you were using it today, you'd probably be being slightly affected or sarcastic: 'Are we going to have the *felicity* of seeing you on Sunday?' has undertones of 'Are you going to condescend to fit us into your busy schedule?' The adjective is *felicitous*, and its opposite means inappropriate, tactless: *an infelicitous remark* is one that leads to an awkward pause in the conversation.

fey

This used to be a serious word, meaning doomed to die or on the point of death; now it's more often used as a disparaging description of someone fanciful and affected, not quite in touch with reality: 'She drifted around the house in that *fey* way of hers, always looking as if she had lost her keys or forgotten how to find her bedroom.'

filigree

A delicate-sounding word for a delicate thing: a form of ornamentation, usually of metalwork or lace: you might twist thin wires of gold or silver together to make *a filigree bracelet*. From the Latin for 'thread', which also gives us *file* and *filament*.

flak

An appropriately brusque little word, abbreviated from the German *Fliegerabwehrkanone*, meaning 'pilot-defence gun'. Like BLITZ, it entered the English language during the Second World War and generally meant anti-aircraft fire, but has since developed the informal sense of strong criticism, fallout when things go wrong, often in the expression *to take the flak*: 'I know I'm sticking my neck out, but I'll take the *flak* if anything goes wrong.'

flaw

A defect or minor fault. It's a common term for an inclusion in a diamond, something that makes it less perfect. But you can also have *flaws* in a fabric such as silk, *character flaws*, *psychological flaws* ... It's an imperfect world. An American actor in the West End might be admired for his *flawless* British accent, but the rare instances of something being described as *flawful* are obviously FLIPPANT, as in a barbed comment in the *Daily News* in 1893: 'Few persons have left flawless poems, but Vaughan's are particularly *flawful*.'

flippant

This originally meant nimble of tongue and was therefore a compliment; somehow it drifted into something less admirable. Much like FACETIOUS, it is now defined as being inappropriately light-hearted, disrespectful of people or subjects that deserve respect: 'I was annoyed by his *flippant* comment, but it did make me wonder if I was taking myself too seriously.'

florid

Connected with *flora* and *floristry*, this originally meant *floral*, abounding with flowers. It then developed to mean two rather different things: *flowery* in a bad, over-the-top sense, so that *florid architecture* and *florid writing* are too fancy and have too many decorative touches; and brightly coloured, specifically *a florid complexion:* red, flushed, the colouring of someone who spends much of their time outdoors or perhaps has high blood pressure.

foible

Related to *feeble*, this is a QUIRK, a little weakness that may be a bit embarrassing but which your friends can regard with affection. The nineteenth- and twentieth-century Canadian physician Sir William Osler explained it perfectly when he observed that 'a library represents the mind of its collector, his fancies and *foibles*, his strength and weakness, his prejudices and preferences.'

footling

The verb *to footle* or *to footle about* means to mess about, to occupy yourself with trivial things; *footling*, the related adjective, means petty, insignificant, not worth bothering about: 'A *footling* query, the sort of thing lawyers ask to make you think they're earning their fee.'

frippery

From an Old French word meaning 'a frill', this can be either ornate and showy clothing, or trivia, or a combination of the two. It can also be an adjective, so that a *frippery* person might care for nothing but clothes, jewellery and other such *fripperies*.

ghoul

'From *ghoulies* and ghosties and long-leggety beasties and things that go bump in the night, Good Lord deliver us,' wrote an anonymous Scottish poet and he meant, of course, *ghouls*, ghosts and long-legged beasts: all scary things that it would be good to be protected against. Of the three, *ghouls*, who take their name from an Arabic word for 'to seize', are probably the most frightening: they are, according to Muslim tradition, spirits that steal human corpses from the grave and eat them. More loosely, they are people who take a morbid delight in unpleasant things: all those massively successful zombie films of recent years appeal to people with a *ghoulish* sense of humour.

glean

Before the invention of farm machinery, a *gleaner* was a person who followed the harvester around, picking up the leftover bits and pieces – it was often the only way they got anything much to eat. Metaphorically, *to glean* is to scrape together a meagre quantity: 'The talk wasn't very interesting, but I *gleaned* what information I could.' Literally or figuratively, *gleaning* is hard work and poorly rewarded.

glitch

Popularized when it was used by American astronaut John Glenn in 1962, this neat little word originally had a technical meaning: a spike or change in voltage in an electrical current, so slight that a fuse couldn't protect against it. It soon – and again thanks to Glenn – broadened to include any technical hitch or snag, often unspecified: 'I can't get online; there's some sort of *glitch* in the broadband connection.'

gloop

A hollow, gulping sound, the sort you might make while ladling thick soup into a bowl or dragging your walking boots out of heavy mud; also the soup or mud itself. A bit like a *plop*, but heavier and thicker. Why? Probably just because it sounds right. See also DOLLOP.

gossamer

This was originally a fine, filmy spider's web; then it became a light, transparent fabric, and can now be anything delicate and flimsy, whether literal or metaphorical. The twentieth-century songwriter Cole Porter referred to a pleasant but short-lived love affair as 'a trip to the moon on *gossamer* wings'. Even more ephemerally and more than half a century later, the novelist Iain Pears described *the gossamer of reputation* as 'so soft and fragile a breath can blow it away'.

grapple

A *grappling iron* or *grappling hook* is a tool with a hook on the end, used as an anchor or to capture an enemy ship in battle or to hook on to anything else that needs to be hooked on to. *To grapple* is used in wrestling, meaning to struggle in a close hold with an opponent, and it can also refer to a mental struggle: a writer (or indeed a reader) of mysteries might *grapple* with the details of a complicated plot.

hubbub

A confused noise, the sort of din made by a lot of people talking at once: 'She couldn't make herself heard above the *hubbub* of voices, so she banged on the table to attract everyone's attention.' Probably from an Irish battle-cry.

humdrum

Routine and monotonous, lacking variety. The not-very-bright movie star played by Jean Hagen in the 1952 film *Singin' in the Rain* says to her audience after a premiere: 'If we bring a little joy into your *hum drum* lives, it makes us feel as though our hard work ain't been in vain for nothing.' She pronounces it as two words, which is how it was first written. Although its origins aren't known for sure, it has a rhythmic repeating pattern in keeping with the unchanging and dull day-to-day activities it describes.

inveigle

Pronounced as if the middle syllable were 'vague', this word has nothing vague about it. It means to trick or lure someone into something: 'The promise of romance *inveigled* customers into buying expensive flowers' or 'He *inveigled* his way into the bridge club by claiming to be a better player than he was.' From an Old French word meaning 'blind'.

irksome

Tedious, troublesome, used to describe something that *irks*. This is often a task: 'Every April I have the *irksome* task of sorting out my accounts.'

irruption

When a volcano *erupts*, lava and other hot stuff break *out* from it; if they were to break *into* it, that would be an *irruption*. Unlikely, of course, with a volcano, but think of the red-caped Monty Python team bursting into the room suddenly and saying, 'Nobody expects the Spanish Inquisition.' That's an *irruption*.

jaunty

Funnily enough, this seems not to be related to a *jaunt*, i.e. a short, pleasurable outing, but is connected with *genteel*: its early meaning was precisely that – well bred and well mannered. Among the characteristics of a *genteel* person were easy good manners, so *jaunty* came to signify smart, self-confident and light-hearted. You might walk *with a jaunty step* if you were feeling cheerful and pleased with yourself; you might also wear your hat *at a jaunty angle*.

jeremiad

Jeremiah was a Hebrew prophet with plenty to complain about, notably his persecution by the Babylonians after they captured and destroyed Jerusalem in the sixth century BC. He wrote the book in the Old Testament that is named after him and he's also credited with writing the one called Lamentations. A *jeremiad*, therefore, is a long, mournful complaint – with the emphasis on the long. Nobody's asking for more by the end of a *jeremiad*.

jolt

Of uncertain origin, a wonderfully abrupt word for an abrupt sensation: a quick shock or jerk that knocks you out of position or off balance. It's particularly applicable to uncomfortable forms of transport and can also be a verb: 'Sitting on the back of the cart, we were *jolted* from side to side as the horse trotted along the uneven track.' *Jolting* can be figurative, too, denoting an unpleasant surprise: 'The election defeat gave him quite a *jolt*: he had expected to win easily.'

jostle
To knock or push against someone, especially in a crowd or a confined space: 'We all *jostled* against each other trying to get through the doorway.' It originally meant to collide with your opponent in a tournament and is related to *joust*.

judder
Possibly a mixture of *jump* or *jar* (in the sense of a clash or harsh vibration) and *shudder*, this is to shake or vibrate intensely, often with reference to something mechanical: 'The aeroplane *juddered* alarmingly before it took off.' Also a noun: 'The engine had a nasty *judder*, but it was safe enough as long as we drove slowly.'

laggard
One who *lags*, loiters, moves annoyingly slowly and doesn't keep up with the rest of the group. The ending *-ard* occurs in a number of words expressing disapproval, to indicate someone who does something discreditable or to excess: a *drunkard* is a person who routinely drinks too much; a *dastard* behaves in a *dastardly* or cowardly way. See also SLUGGISH.

lassitude

Tiredness. But tiredness of a weary, indifferent, can't-drag-yourself-out-of-bed, can't-be-bothered-to-do-anything kind. Interestingly, according to the ancient Chinese philosopher Confucius, it's a condition that can be cured by tea which, he says, 'tempers the spirits and harmonizes the mind, dispels *lassitude* and relieves fatigue'. What better excuse for a tea break?

listless

Nothing to do with the sort of *list* you might take with you when you go shopping or with a ship *listing to starboard*; this means lacking in *list*, in the archaic sense of delight, longing, inclination – any of the pleasurable emotions that make you look forward to each new day. A *listless* person lolls about on the sofa or flits from task to task without enthusiasm or energy. They don't even have the excuse of being depressed – they're just bereft of any zest for life.

luxuriate

Imagine yourself in a warm, scented bath or surrounded by the softest of cushions or the crispest of linen sheets. You're in no hurry: you can *luxuriate* in your surroundings for as long as you like. When you're enjoying *luxury* or indulging in something *luxurious*, what you are doing is *luxuriating*.

mayhem

A variant of *maim* rather than anything to do with the month of *May,* this means chaos, noisy confusion: 'It's always *mayhem* at the end of term – we have loads of paperwork to do and the kids are completely overexcited.'

morass

A tract of swampy land or, figuratively, a set of circumstances in which you get bogged down: 'She lost herself in a *morass* of lies and deception.'

motley

In medieval times, court jesters dressed in multicoloured costumes called *motley*, and the word has come to be an adjective that describes anything made up of diverse elements, whether fabrics, colours or individuals in a group: 'A *motley* collection of aspiring actors turned up for the audition.'

nuzzle

A funny word, etymologically speaking – it's like snuggling with your nose (see SNUGGLE). It originally meant to burrow or dig with your nose, to investigate with your nose or to nose around for fodder, something you were unlikely to do unless you were a pig or a truffle hound. Then it became more affectionate – you could *nuzzle up against someone's shoulder*, for example, burying your nose (and indeed the rest of your face) in it. From there it developed two wider uses: you can now *nuzzle down in bed*, making yourself snug and warm there; or you can *nuzzle up to someone* or *nuzzle together with them*, nestling, cuddling, generally being cosy and close. It doesn't seem to have anything to do with *muzzle*, though you can't help feeling it should.

plangent
Having a loud, deep, mournful sound, from a Latin word meaning 'to beat the breast in grief' (who knew the Romans had a word for that?). Often used in a musical context, such as *the plangent notes of the cello* or *his plangent, bluesy voice*.

quail
What you do when you shrink away from someone or something that frightens you: 'I *quailed* at the prospect of making a speech at the wedding.' Of unknown origin; nothing to do with the game bird.

quirk
A characteristic, an idiosyncrasy, often harmless, possibly even endearing, but odd. You can have a *quirk of speech, a quirk of fate* or *a quirky way of dressing* – it doesn't matter, as long as it's a bit peculiar. See also FOIBLE.

qui vive

Pronounced 'key veeve', this is taken from a French sentry's call to someone approaching the guard post; it means '(Long) live who?' or 'Whose side are you on?' In English, it's used only in the expression *on the qui vive*, meaning on the alert, on the lookout: 'My senses were on the *qui vive* as I walked across the dark park.'

scamper

To run, in a busy, swift, playful way. You can *scamper through a task,* with the implication that you have skimped it and not done it properly, but mostly *scampering* summons up visions of children or small dogs running up and down stairs or through the long grass in a park. Definitely something to be done off the leash.

scuttle

A word with three separate meanings from three separate sources: there's a container for coal; a way of sinking one's own ship; and the rather endearing one, which is to run with short, hasty steps, like a rabbit or a nervous person: 'She didn't want to talk to anyone, so she *scuttled* away to make the tea.' Related to the more confident *scud*, which is how clouds move across the sky on a windy day.

seep

What liquid does when it drips, filters or oozes slowly but surely through somewhere that you don't want it to be, leaving a feeling of cold, damp and misery. The novelist Elizabeth Bowen wrote in the late 1930s about some London houses that had been converted into gloomy little hotels: 'Their builders must have built to enclose fog, which having *seeped* in never quite goes away.'

sepulchral

Pertaining to a *sepulchre*, a grand tomb, from the Latin word for 'to bury': you might find a room in *sepulchral darkness* if no one had bothered to open the curtains. Also often used metaphorically to mean gloomy, melancholy, perhaps with reference to a deep, resonant voice, such as *the sepulchral tones of the veteran radio announcer.*

skulk

Of Scandinavian origin, *to skulk* is to *lurk* somewhere you won't be seen or to move stealthily so as not to be noticed: 'He was *skulking* in the alleyway waiting for me to come home.' *Lurk* is from Middle English, but the two can be used more or less interchangeably.

slather

To spread generously – with something reasonably thick such as cream, soap or perhaps, as in the case of the lobster mentioned under AMBROSIA, mayonnaise. It doesn't much matter, as long as the result is luxurious and slightly messy.

sloth

Which came first, the animal or the deadly sin? According to the *OED*, the sin – idleness, laziness, disinclination to do anything that requires effort – wins by about 500 years, but even so the animal dates back to the early seventeenth century and is named because of its SLUGGISH disposition. It moves through the trees (when it has to) as if in slow motion and comes to the ground to relieve itself about once a week. British English has the right idea with this word – it pronounces it with a long 'o' (as in 'slow', from which it is in part derived), which sounds a lot lazier than the brisker, shorter-vowelled American version.

sluggish

'Go to the ant, thou *sluggard*; consider her ways and be wise,' advises the Old Testament book of Proverbs. In other words, follow the example of someone hardworking and stop being so lazy yourself. A *sluggard* (or someone of a *sluggish* disposition) is habitually idle and loafs about or *slugs* – the word referred to a lazy person long before it became a garden pest. It also gave us the gorgeous *slug-a-bed,* someone who hates getting up in the morning. It's not only people who are *sluggish*: an elderly vehicle might *chug sluggishly up the hill*. See also LAGGARD.

slump

Originally meaning to fall heavily into water or mud (and probably coined in imitation of the sound that such an activity makes); now more likely to refer to falling heavily into an armchair and sitting there *in a slumped position*, the opposite of upright. Stock markets can (and do) *slump* when prices fall sharply and *an economic slump* is a small step away from a depression.

smarmy

A nasty-sounding word for a nasty concept: it means flattering or complimentary in an unpleasant way. In the nineteenth century, *smarm* was a dialect word for to smear; in the twentieth, its specific meaning was to slick your hair down with gel or cream, so that when *smarmy* was applied to a person or their manners, it meant unattractively oily. *Oleaginous*, from the Latin for 'of the olive tree' (and its oil), means much the same thing and is equally creepy. See also UNCTUOUS.

snuggle

To make yourself *snug* – comfortably warm, possibly wrapped up in something soft or close to someone you're fond of: 'We *snuggled* up together in front of the fire' or 'It was so *snug* in the cottage that it was easy to ignore the storm outside.' In old-fashioned British pubs (including *Coronation Street*'s Rovers Return), a *snug* is a small, cosy bar with room for very few people. See also NUZZLE.

sodden

Saturated with water or some other moisture; it can be applied to anything from boggy ground to a towel you haven't wrung out properly. When used of a person, it means having the characteristics that this might imply: being stupid and dull, often through drunkenness (you might be *gin-sodden* or *whisky-sodden*, depending on your tastes). *Soggy*, a word with a similarly engrained feeling of squelchiness, doesn't usually refer to the effects of alcohol or tearfulness, but anyone who watches television baking programmes knows how undesirable a *soggy bottom* is.

squeamish

Likely to feel sick, uncomfortable or frightened at anything from the sight of blood to a spider in the bath or an unpleasant story in the media: 'I'm a bit *squeamish* about anything to do with needles.' Of obscure origin, but with the implication that you are overreacting.

succulent

Deliciously juicy, either literally – *a succulent slice of melon* – or more broadly – *a succulent piece of steak* or even *a succulent morsel of gossip.* As a noun, a *succulent* is a type of plant, such as a cactus, which stores water in its stem and leaves.

susurration

A poetic word for whispering, either the pleasant sound of a light wind rustling the trees or the less welcome one of gossip. The essayist Charles Lamb, confiding some news to a friend in 1825, wrote: 'I cannot be more explicit at present ... Not a *susurration* of this to *anybody*!'

svelte

A French word meaning not only slim, but sleek, elegant and graceful with it. Although you would usually apply it to a woman, you could also admire *the svelte lines of a Rolls-Royce* or *the svelte outline of Seattle's Space Needle.*

torrid

Extremely hot and dry, from the Latin for 'to scorch'. It can be used literally – *the torrid climate of the Sahara* – or figuratively, with reference to passionate moments in a film – *a torrid sex scene.*

tousled

Often relating to hair or general appearance, dishevelled, untidy, unkempt: 'She had that *tousled* look of someone who had slept through the alarm and dressed in a hurry.' From Old English and German words meaning 'to handle roughly', 'to pull about'.

truck

Truck meaning commercial goods or dealings has nothing to do with *truck* in the sense of a lorry or a railway vehicle. The former probably comes from an Old French word for 'to barter' and it's from here that we get the expression *to have no truck with* someone or something: to refuse to have dealings with someone or be involved with something because you disapprove: 'She had no *truck* with old-fashioned etiquette – she refused to curtsey to anyone.'

trundle

This feels as if it ought to be a portmanteau word (see GALUMPH) – a combination of 'trudge' and 'bundle', perhaps – but sadly it isn't: it's from an Old French word for 'to bowl or roll along', and that is what it originally meant. Back in the days when children bowled hoops along the pavement as a form of entertainment, *trundling* was another word for what they were doing to the hoop. Since then, it's come to mean to move heavily, usually on wheels: you might *trundle a wheelbarrow*, perhaps, or *trundle along the country roads* in an old-fashioned bus. Trundling is definitely ungainly, though: you can't do it in a Porsche or a Lamborghini.

unctuous

Literally oily or greasy (related to the *unction* or anointing with oil that is part of some Christian rites); more often oily or greasy in manner, SMARMY: 'He had a certain *unctuous* charm, but I could never believe he was sincere.'

unkempt

Kempt comes originally from *kemb*, an old word for 'to comb'; especially to draw a comb through a horse's tangled mane. To be *kempt*, therefore, is to be combed, well groomed, generally tidy, particularly with reference to the hair and beard. *Unkempt* is quite the reverse, and can refer not just to a person's appearance, but also to a garden (*unkempt flower beds* haven't been weeded lately), a building (*unkempt brickwork* is in need of repointing) or anything else that looks as if it would benefit from some TLC.

wallow

The once hugely popular 'Hippopotamus Song', recorded in 1960 by Michael Flanders and Donald Swann, features the lyric 'let us *wallow* in glorious mud', and that is what an animal such as a hippo does: lies or rolls in something wet and/or messy and thoroughly enjoys itself. The word also exists as a noun to describe a mud-hole or dust-hole formed by a heavy animal doing just that. But you don't need mud – nor do you need to be a hippopotamus or a buffalo – in order to wallow: you can *wallow in nostalgia* by watching a favourite old film or *wallow in your own misery* by lying in bed all day crying and eating chocolate. You may find that the hippo's version is more fun, though.

wangle

To achieve something in a way that isn't entirely honest or by the book: 'I *wangled* a long weekend by phoning in sick on Friday morning' or 'He *wangled* his way into the job on the basis of three weeks' internship and an upper-class accent.' Of uncertain origin and not to be confused with *to wrangle,* which means to debate something noisily or publicly – 'The neighbours were always *wrangling* over who was allowed to park in front of the house' – or, in American English, to be a *wrangler*, someone in charge of a string of horses on a ranch.

whimsy

A quaint, fantastic idea or humour, not rooted in common sense or practicality; the kind that would lead to you doing something on a *whim*, because the mood suddenly took you and you didn't stop to think it through: 'There was a touch of *whimsy* about the decor, all floating fabrics and fragile china ornaments.' The rather *whimsical* alternatives *whim-wham* and *whimsy-whamsy* have never been in common use, but are available to anyone who fancies reviving them.

winsome

Pretty in appearance and/or agreeable in manner: *a winsome smile* or *a winsome little girl*. There's a feeling of peacefulness about it, but also the suggestion of being too good to be true. From Old English; not related to *winning* in the modern sense.

wistful

Sadly thoughtful; longing for something that might have been or that has been and is no more: 'She spoke *wistfully* of the house she had lived in as a child.' *Wistful* has another, obsolete meaning of paying close attention, and may therefore come from an old adverb *wistly*, meaning attentively. There seems never to have been a noun *wist*, meaning the sort of thing a *wistful* look might be full of, but there is a rarely used adjective *wistless*, meaning inattentive.

wizened

Old and shrivelled; used of plants, animals and people. You might find *a wizened apple* fallen from a tree or describe a very elderly person as having *a wizened face* (or COUNTENANCE, if you were feeling poetical – the two words go well together). It's not much of a compliment, though, so probably better not to say it to their face. Or countenance.

woebegone

Forlorn, afflicted with *woe* or misery. Look at a dog that has just realized you are not about to take it for a walk and you'll see a living, breathing portrait of *woebegoneness.*

wombat

When you start analysing what qualifies a word as beautiful, this may not be one that comes immediately to mind, but it fits perfectly into the category of 'exactly right for its purpose': a short, chunky word for a short, chunky creature. A wombat is, of course, a burrowing Australian marsupial with short legs, powerful claws and sharp teeth, and the name is simply an anglicization of its indigenous one. It would be nice to think that it came from an Aboriginal word for 'short and chunky', but sadly there's no evidence for that.

yomp

A splendidly onomatopoeic word for walking across difficult terrain, probably heavily laden and wearing boots that pick up more and more mud as you go. Originally military slang, it gained wider currency during the Falklands War of 1982; by June of that year, a reporter for the *Observer* newspaper, covering a Scottish by-election, was able to refer to '*yomping* round the sodden and trackless wastes of the constituency'. The point is that whether you are doing it in the South Atlantic or a Labour stronghold on the outskirts of Glasgow, *yomping* is hard work.

zephyr
Say it lightly enough and it sounds like a gentle breeze – which is precisely what it is. In Classical times it was specifically the west wind, but nowadays a *zephyr* can blow softly from any direction.

CHAPTER TWO

Words That Sound Clever

Loving words isn't the same thing as showing off your vocabulary: you don't always want people to be speechless with admiration or to wonder what on earth you are talking about. However, there may be times …

abstemious

All five vowels, once only and in alphabetical order
– there aren't many words of which that can be said (see
FACETIOUS for another). That orthographic curiosity apart,
it means sparing, self-denying, not inclined to eat, drink,
spend or indulge in anything very much. There's nothing
wrong with that: an *abstemious* person isn't necessarily
either miserly or holier-than-thou, they're just not very
good at letting their hair down. *Abstinent* – related to
abstain and *abstinence* – is slightly different. If you *abstain*
from something (often sex), you don't indulge at all;
abstemiousness merely implies moderation.

acclivity

An upward slope, an incline. The opposite of a *declivity*,
which is by definition heading downhill. An 1838
description of London's Highgate Cemetery, which occupies
a hilly site, remarks that the landscaping has made the
space look larger than it is: 'This effect is produced by
circuitous roads, winding about the *acclivity*, not only
making the ascent more gradual but greatly increasing
the distance.' The unknown author of this piece, published
in the wonderfully named *The Mirror of Literature,
Amusement and Instruction,* obviously approved: he went
on to say that the eye would LUXURIATE on a variety of
objects and elegant monuments.

accolade

There's an obsolete verb *accoll*, meaning to throw your
arms round somebody's neck, and an *accolade* was

originally a greeting of this sort. Then it became the action of dubbing someone a knight by tapping a sword on his shoulders. Both words are connected with the Old French *col*, meaning 'neck', from which we also get *collar*. Nowadays, any wholehearted mark of approval, from a glowing review of an actor's performance to awarding a physicist a Nobel Prize, can be described as an *accolade*, often accompanied by the grandiose verb *bestow*, which maintains some of the medieval pomp of the original meaning.

acumen

Sharpness, especially intellectual sharpness; the ability to cut through VERBIAGE and get to the point: 'With infuriating *acumen*, she realized he was making excuses to cover up his inefficiency.' It derives from the Latin for 'needle' and is related to *acute* and *acupuncture*. You might think it should also be related to *accurate*, but this (spelled with two cs, note) comes from a word meaning 'performed with care' and is connected to *cure*.

ancillary

Subsidiary, auxiliary, as in *ancillary forces* that are sent into battle to supplement the main ones. Also a noun, meaning a person serving *an ancillary function*: 'We have an *ancillary* in Nice, but he refers big decisions to the Paris office.' From the Latin for 'a maidservant', though the modern word makes no assumptions about gender.

anomaly

From a Greek word meaning 'uneven' or 'irregular', an *anomaly* is something that differs from the norm and is out of place in the situation in which you find it: 'Her dark hair was an *anomaly* in a family of redheads' or 'There was an *anomaly* in the sales figures – the range seemed to have sold well in the south-west, but nowhere else.'

aphorism

A wise saying, briefly and neatly phrased: 'Blessed is he who expects nothing, for he shall never be disappointed' or 'Fools rush in where angels fear to tread.' These were both coined by the eighteenth-century English poet Alexander Pope, though the word comes from the Greek for 'a definition' and was first used by Hippocrates, the Ancient Greek 'Father of Medicine', as a title for his compilation of propositions about symptoms, diagnosis and treatment. The concept spread across the globe and down the ages; other notable aphorists include the German philosopher Friedrich Nietzsche, the Irish playwright Oscar Wilde and the American wit Dorothy Parker.

apocryphal

Unproven, unlikely to be true, from the Greek for 'to hide away'. In Christian teaching, the *Apocrypha* consists of fourteen books that are included in some versions of the Bible but excluded from others on the grounds that they are not *canonical* – not proper, authoritative scripture. From this we get the idea of a story being *apocryphal*, like the six-year-old George Washington cutting down a cherry tree and owning up to his father because he couldn't tell a lie. It's been much repeated, it seems entirely in character, but it probably didn't happen.

apparatchik

From the Russian for *apparatus*, the means by which something operates, this is a member of the *apparat*, the organization of the Communist Party of the former Soviet Union; and thence a bureaucrat, a cog in any political or civil-service machine. Like bureaucrat, *apparatchik* implies pernickety attention to detail rather than dynamic policy-making.

arrogate

Related to *arrogant* and similarly self-centred, this means to claim without justification, to reserve for yourself: 'I *arrogate* to myself the right to criticize my husband; I don't let anyone else do it.'

asseverate

To affirm, assert, aver – to insist strongly that something is so: 'He *asseverated* that he had been nowhere near the scene of the accident.' There's no messing about when you're *asseverating*: it's a serious word, related to *severe*.

astringent

From the Latin for 'drawing together', this is applied to a drug, ointment or the like that causes the body's tissues to contract, stemming the flow of blood or other fluids. Adapt that to a figurative sense and you have sharp, severe, stern. Thus, blackcurrants have *an astringent quality*, but so does the voice of someone who is taking you firmly to task: uttering no threats, but leaving you in no doubt that they are displeased.

attrition

Continual wearing down of strength or effectiveness in order to weaken or destroy; gradual reduction. Often in the expression *a war of attrition*, the sort of war that consists of a number of small battles rather than one massive encounter. *A war of attrition* can also take place on a sports field, where one team relentlessly plugs away at the other's defence, or in the home, where whining or sulking may eventually wear down parental discipline and let a child have its own way.

bailiwick

Strictly, the area under the jurisdiction of a *bailiff*, a medieval official roughly equivalent to a sheriff. More loosely, it's a person's area of expertise, field of authority or comfort zone: 'I'm outside my *bailiwick* here – I've never done this sort of thing before.'

bibliophile

Biblio- is to do with books (as in *bibliography*, a list of books, and the *Bible*, from the Greek for 'the books') and *-phile* means someone who loves – see ARCTOPHILE. Thus, a *bibliophile* is simply someone who loves books. Nothing wrong with that, obviously; if you want to suggest that there *is* something wrong with it or that the person in question is taking their hobby a bit too far, you could call them a *bibliomaniac* instead.

Brobdingnagian

In Jonathan Swift's 1726 novel *Gulliver's Travels*, Brobdingnag is a fictional country that is peopled by giants, so the adjective derived from it means gigantic, enormous: 'I wasn't hungry, but my companion ate a meal of *Brobdingnagian* proportions.' The opposite is *Lilliputian*, tiny, from another place that Gulliver visits; the inhabitants of *Lilliput* are so small that they think Gulliver is a giant.

cabal

Derived from *Kabbalah*, a Jewish tradition based on a certain interpretation of the Old Testament, this evolved to mean, first, any esoteric tradition and then more generally an intrigue, a secret plot. By the late seventeenth century, it had also come to refer to a small group of people indulging in such an intrigue, helped on its way by the happy coincidence that Charles II's Privy Council included five ministers called Clifford, Arlington, Buckingham, Ashley and Lauderdale. Nowadays, you might find *a cabal of businessmen* or *a cabal of bankers* engaged in some CHICANERY, possibly illegal and certainly lacking transparency.

captious

Fault-finding, ready to take offence at trivial things. Lord Chesterfield, the eighteenth-century aristocrat whom we met under DESPONDENT, described it rather neatly when he wrote: 'A vulgar man is *captious* and jealous; eager and impetuous about trifles. He suspects himself to be slighted, [and] thinks everything that is said [is] meant at him.'

cautionary

Carrying a *caution*, as in Hilaire Belloc's *Cautionary Tales for Children* (1907). In this improving work, the youthful reader is warned of the dire consequences of lying (you get burned to death), being a cry-baby (you ruin your chances of a political career), running away from your nurse (you get eaten by a lion) and other misdemeanours likely to occur to a spirited child.

cavalcade

A procession, strictly speaking of people on horseback (from the Latin for 'horse' and related to *cavalier*), though it can be applied loosely to any festive and/or dignified parade. Noël Coward's 1931 play *Cavalcade* is a vast patriotic epic boasting a 400-strong cast; the film adaptation, which won the Oscar for Best Picture in 1933, has plenty of horses, too. Coward later remarked that before he wrote the play 'the word had fallen into disuse. Now there are ... *Cavalcades* of fashion, Hollywood *Cavalcades* ... *Cavalcades* of practically anything that can be *cavalcaded*.'

circuitous

Going in a *circuit*, taking a roundabout way to a destination, whether it be *a circuitous route* to the centre of town or *a circuitous piece of reasoning* to arrive at a conclusion. Despite being spelled like the two-syllable *circuit* (pronounced 'sir-kit'), this comes out as four syllables: 'sir-queue-it-us'.

circumspect

Literally looking around, but used in the figurative sense of being cautious or prudent, considering all the options before you make a decision. A tabloid newspaper may report an item with brash, sweeping statements, while a thoughtful monthly magazine is more *circumspect*; you could also be *circumspect* about where you went for lunch with a colleague if you didn't want the rest of the team to see you together.

circumvent

Anything beginning with *circum-* is likely to be about going around (see CIRCUMSPECT) and the *vent* part here comes from the Latin for 'to come'. *To circumvent* is not so much to *come* round as to *get* round – particularly to get round the rules, to get the better of something: 'He *circumvented* the plan to dismiss him by making sure no one else could access the bank account.'

cogitate

To think very deeply. The seventeenth-century French philosopher René Descartes famously wrote, '*Cogito, ergo sum*' – I think, therefore I am – and *cogitate* comes from the first word in this Latin phrase. It's nothing to do with the cog that makes a wheel go round but, by a pleasing coincidence, *cogitation* is the sort of thought that makes you imagine you can hear mental cogs grinding.

collude

The Latin root of this word means 'to play together', but in English it is to conspire together, to plan something underhand: 'The directors of the various companies *colluded* to keep pay levels as low as possible.' There are certain contexts in business in which *collusion* contravenes competition or anti-trust laws and is therefore illegal; even when it's not, it's dishonourable.

conceit

This is, of course, that unendearing quality akin to vanity, but it has a literary sense, too: it means a far-fetched comparison, a fanciful notion. A nineteenth-century analysis of Greek poetry cited by the *OED* has this withering comparison with the florid style that was fashionable at the time: 'The Greeks had no *conceits*: they did not call the waves "nodding hearse-plumes" ... or laburnums "dropping wells of fire".' But *conceit* may also be used in a neutral sense: if you said that a book of verse used the *conceit* of arranging the poems according to theme rather than chronologically, you wouldn't necessarily be suggesting that this was a pretentious thing to do.

conflagration

A large, destructive fire, the kind that will burn a house or a forest to the ground. It can also be used figuratively of, for example, the sort of intense passions that stir up a revolution.

conspicuous

Clearly visible, standing out from a crowd: 'That yellow jacket made him very *conspicuous*.' Often found in the sardonic expression 'he was *conspicuous* by his absence', suggesting that he stayed away out of cowardice or because he knew he wouldn't be welcome or with some similar subtext.

contingency

Something that may happen, but probably won't, often in the expression *a remote contingency*. A *contingency plan* is drawn up 'just in case', but is unlikely to be needed.

corporeal

Of the body. That means both solid – having a physical existence – and mortal, as opposed to *ethereal*, of the air, very light; or *spiritual*, relating to the soul or spirit, or to the Church. From the Latin *corpus*, meaning 'a body', which also gives us the idea of a *corpus* or body of work, the total collected writings (usually by various people) on a given subject. An individual's output is more likely to be described by the French word *oeuvre*, meaning 'work'.

critique

Not to be confused with a *criticism*, which is an unfavourable comment, a *critique* is an analysis or review, usually of something artistic or literary, and may be favourable, unfavourable or neutral: 'His *critique* of the exhibition made it sound more interesting than I'd expected.'

culminate

From a Latin word meaning 'the top or highest point', *to culminate* is to reach an end, usually with a sense of climax or disaster: 'The production *culminated* in a spectacular dance routine' or 'Her refusal to turn down work *culminated* in our having to cancel our holiday.'

cursive

At the start of a long-ago episode of the television series *The Simpsons*, Bart is seen writing on the chalkboard: '*Cursive* writing does not mean what I think it does.' And he is quite right: *cursive* is from the Latin for 'to run' and *cursive writing* is joined-up writing, written with a running hand. The word isn't often found in any other context and certainly has nothing to do with cursing.

cynosure

In 1922, the great authority on American etiquette, Emily Post, published her collected wisdom in a book called *Etiquette in Society, in Business, in Politics and at Home.* That informative title should perhaps also have included 'in the Field of Sport', because she gives this invaluable advice on riding clothes: 'Have your breeches fit you. The coat is less important, in fact, any odd coat will do. Your legs are the *cynosure* of attention in riding.' She means that they are the centre of attention, the part of you that will attract admiration. A more precise meaning for *cynosure* (literally 'dog's tail') is 'something that acts as a guide', because it comes from the Greek name for the constellation *Ursa Minor,* which includes the Pole Star and therefore serves as a guide to navigators without access to modern technology.

deportment

From Latin and French words for 'to carry' and 'to carry away', this is related to *deporting* someone from a country where they have been denied the right to stay. The act of doing that is *deportation*. But *deportment* means the way you carry yourself or behave yourself: young ladies at finishing school used to attend *deportment classes*, during which they were taught to walk elegantly by balancing a book on top of their head. More generally, it can mean not much more than look or manner, and it doesn't have to be elegant: 'His whole *deportment* was shifty, as if he were anxious not to be seen.'

depredation

The act of plunder or looting, related to *predator* and *prey*, and often used in the plural. It can be literal and serious – 'The settlements on the steppes suffered *depredation* at the hands of the Mongol hordes'; less literal but still serious – 'global warming has made severe *depredations* into the polar ice caps'; or less literal and a bit frivolous – 'I see you've made great *depredations* into that box of chocolates while I've been out.'

desideratum

Something very much desired or needed: the nineteenth-century essayist Charles Lamb wrote on the subject of books that 'to be strong-backed and neat-bound is the *desideratum* of a volume. Magnificence comes after.' The plural is *desiderata*, which is also the title of the famous 1927 prose poem by Max Ehrmann that begins 'Go placidly amid the noise and haste' and goes on to list many other desirable things.

None of this is to be confused with a *desiderium,* which is a desire for something that is missed or lost, an extra-sad form of nostalgia: 'The *desiderium* I felt for my student days made it painful for me to attend reunions.'

elliptical

In grammar, an *ellipsis* is symbolized by three dots (...) and used to indicate that something is missing or that a speaker has tailed off without finishing what they were going to say. If you needed an adjective to describe that, it would be *elliptical,* which can also be used in a figurative sense, to mean indirect and inexplicit: 'He made an *elliptical* reference to moving house, but I didn't realize he was leaving the country.'

embargo

A Spanish word for 'a ban' or 'prohibition', often a legal order: 'There was a strict *embargo* on wines and spirits being shipped through the port.' As a verb, it's also used in journalism: 'The news was *embargoed* until noon on Thursday', meaning it wasn't to be published before then.

embryonic

Like an *embryo*, a plant, animal or concept in a very early stage of development (in human terms, the *embryo* lasts for about the first eight weeks of pregnancy, before it becomes known as a *foetus*). So, *an embryonic idea* is something that needs to be worked on and developed before you can call it a proposal or a plan. A historian might also refer to the *embryonic stock exchange* of the Middle Ages – not a stock exchange in the modern sense, but an early form of it that laid the foundations of what we know today.

eminent

Distinguished, standing out from the crowd, especially by virtue of long service: you might speak of *an eminent professor*, for example, or *an eminent scientist*. It comes from the Latin for 'to project' and is not to be confused with *imminent*, which means likely to happen in the near future – a heavily pregnant woman expects to give birth *imminently*.

emissary

An agent, a person sent on behalf of someone else – from the Latin for 'to send out' and related to *mission*. An *emissary*'s task is likely to be to gather information, to plead a cause or possibly to make apologies that you are too embarrassed to make in person.

expiate

To atone or make amends for, frequently in a religious context – the thing you *expiate* is often a sin. The middle part is connected with *piety*, with the same implication of religious duty or devotion.

exposition

Related to *expose* and *exposure*, this is the action of putting something on public display or of setting out an idea or theory in speech or writing: 'The lawyer's *exposition* was masterly – no one was in any doubt about the logic of his argument.' The first international fairs, designed in the nineteenth century to display the achievements of the countries involved and now usually known merely as *expos*, were also *expositions*.

extant

Surviving, still in existence: 'Aristophanes wrote forty plays, but only eleven are *extant*.' It's slightly different from simply existing: *extant* has the additional sense of having survived – it can be applied to an animal wrongly thought to be extinct, as well as to Greek plays that are still with us almost 2,500 years on.

extempore

Impromptu, off the cuff, spoken or performed without preparation or rehearsal. From the Latin for 'out of the time'. *Extemporaneous* can mean the same thing, or it can be more like improvised, made up on the spot to solve a problem but not intended as a long-term answer. In both cases – whether giving *an extempore speech* or providing *an extemporaneous solution* – what you are doing is *extemporizing*.

extenuate

From the Latin for 'to make thin', this is to make something appear less serious than it is, to moderate: 'I tried to *extenuate* his annoyance by explaining why I hadn't finished my assignment.' Often found in the expression *extenuating circumstances*, meaning circumstances that excuse you from doing something you shouldn't have done.

fealty

Loyalty, allegiance, specifically the allegiance a vassal owed to his overlord in feudal times. Not often used in a non-historical context, but an art student might acknowledge *fealty* to Pablo Picasso, say, or an aspiring poet to Carol Ann Duffy.

feasible

Possible, doable: 'The work sounds straightforward enough, but I don't think the schedule is *feasible*.' Hence the *feasibility study* frequently carried out in the workplace in an attempt to assess in advance whether or not a new system or business model is a good idea.

fecundity

From the Latin for 'fertile', this is fruitfulness, the quality of a soil that produces a lavish quantity of crops or a woman who produces a vast number of children. Alternatively, it can refer to artistic or intellectual achievement: 'The Age of Enlightenment owes its name to the remarkable *fecundity* of philosophical and scientific thought of the period.' The adjective *fecund* is less pleasing to the ear, but still sounds quite clever.

fruition

Often in the expression *to come to fruition*, this means a satisfactory conclusion, the happy result of hard work: 'At last his plans have come to *fruition* and he can afford to set up a business of his own.' From the Latin for 'enjoyment' and related to *fruit*, but pronounced as three syllables – 'froo-ish-un'.

fugacious
Fleeting, lasting only a very short time. From the Latin for 'to flee' and related to *fugitive*, it's a poetic word, not common in modern speech: the nineteenth-century social theorist Harriet Martineau wrote of 'the *fugacious* nature of life and time', and you might also apply it to scents, short-lived flowers or a glimpse of something disappearing into the undergrowth.

furtive
Secretive, stealthy, often for shameful or criminal reasons: it derives from the Latin for 'a thief'. A small animal might be *furtive* without evil intent – the novelist and poet Thomas Hardy wrote of a hedgehog travelling '*furtively* over the lawn' – but a person doing the same thing is definitely hoping not to be noticed. It isn't only movement that can be furtive; you might have *a furtive look on your face* if you had been caught somewhere you shouldn't have been.

harbinger
A forerunner, a person or thing that announces the approach of something. Often in an alarming way, as in *a harbinger of doom/disaster*. Oddly, the word's origins are distinctly comfortable: it's related to *harbour* and an early

definition of *harbinger* was a person sent ahead of a royal party or army to make sure that suitable accommodation was ready for them.

hauteur

This is the everyday French word for 'height': a person who is 1.8 metres tall is said to have *1.8 mètres de hauteur*, with no suggestion of approval or disapproval. In English, though, it means haughtiness, an unpleasantness of manner that gives the impression you are looking down on someone: 'She smiled and shook my hand, but with a certain *hauteur* that didn't make me feel welcome.'

ideation

The power of the mind to create new ideas, usually those not apparent to the senses. A psychologist might talk of the individual's *ideation of reality* (not the same as a strictly rational world view) or you could have *ideations of new markets* (not yet fulfilled) in order to expand your business.

impasse

The French word for 'cul-de-sac' or 'dead end', this has a figurative meaning in English: a deadlock, a position from which there is no going forward. Often used to describe negotiations that have failed to achieve a result: 'The talks have reached an *impasse*.' You can, if you like, pronounce the first syllable in the French way (more 'am' than 'im'), but the English way (to rhyme with 'him') is OK, too.

implacable

Unable to be *placated* or pacified; inflexible, not about to change your mind or your attitude: 'They were *implacable* enemies and were never going to come together at a negotiating table.'

impolitic

Not *politic*, not wise or prudent, particularly for the time being or in the present circumstances: 'It would be *impolitic* to ask for time off in December when the shop is so busy.'

imprimatur

Latin for 'let it be printed', this is a – literal or metaphorical – seal of approval. Historically, it referred to the Roman Catholic Church giving permission for a book to be published; nowadays it can be used more loosely, as in 'The building work couldn't begin without the *imprimatur* of the school board.'

impunity

Without danger of being *punished*, or having the good fortune to avoid *punishment*: 'Hoodlums roam the streets with *impunity* because there aren't enough police to keep them under control.'

inalienable
An adjective describing something that cannot be made *alien*; in other words, that can't be taken away or transferred to someone else. Most famously, the US Declaration of Independence speaks of 'certain *unalienable* Rights, that among these are Life, Liberty and the pursuit of Happiness'.

incarnadine
Related to *incarnate* (as in *the Devil incarnate*, the Devil made flesh), this means blood red, crimson. There's a great quote from Shakespeare's *Macbeth*, spoken by Macbeth himself after he's committed his first murder:

> *Will all great Neptune's ocean wash this blood*
> *Clean from my hand? No, this my hand will rather*
> *The multitudinous seas incarnardine,*
> *Making the green one red.*

Meaning that there's enough blood on my hands to turn the oceans red. That's a lot of blood. Shakespeare is using *incarnadine* as a verb, meaning to turn something red; you're probably safer sticking to the adjective and using it to describe a sunset or a field of poppies rather than your hands after you've murdered someone.

incipient
Beginning, coming into being, at an early stage. It can describe all sorts of things, from medical conditions (*incipient dementia*) to feelings (*an incipient panic at*

the approach of exams). The implication is that both the dementia and the panic are likely to develop further as time goes by.

incisive
Cutting, as with a sharp blade – related to the *incision* a surgeon might make with a scalpel. But *incisiveness* can apply to figurative cuts as well, arising from intelligent analysis and clear thinking: *an incisive remark* cuts to the essence of the debate, while making *an incisive decision* means that you stop discussing whatever it is and start doing something about it.

incongruous
Congruent is a term in maths describing a balanced relationship between two integers: it's from a Latin word meaning 'to meet together', 'to agree'. So anything *congruous* is suitable, appropriate, in harmony with its surroundings or circumstances. It's less commonly used than its opposite, *incongruous*, which means out of place, inappropriate, discordant: 'Her pink hat seemed an *incongruous* choice for a funeral' or 'His tremendous height made him look *incongruous* in his school photo, as if he had accidentally wandered into a younger class.'

incremental
An *increment* is an increase, particularly when it forms part of a series – a pay rise that is calculated as a percentage of

your current wages, for example: 'An annual *increment* of three per cent.' *Incremental* is the adjective that describes something increasing in this way: 'We can't expect miracles, but we can hope for *incremental* improvements over a period of time.'

indigent

Poor, needy, from the Latin for 'to lack': 'Providing free education for *indigent* children (or children in *indigent* circumstances) was unheard of before the nineteenth century.'

indubitable

Unable to be doubted, having nothing *dubious* about it. Despite its tongue-twisting qualities, it is usually used in formal contexts: 'It was the clear and *indubitable* truth' or 'He had an *indubitable* right to be present at the trial.'

ineluctable

Unescapable, from the Latin for 'to struggle out'. As so often, it doesn't have to be literal: a charismatic person might cast *an ineluctable spell* over anyone who came their way.

infiltrate

To penetrate by *filtration*, to sneak into a place or an organization like a liquid passing through something porous. Often used in a military context, as in *infiltrating the enemy camp*, but also in a wider sense: 'Textspeak and even emojis are *infiltrating* more formal writing.'

ingenuous

Candid, frank, free from any form of slyness: the characteristics of an *ingénue*, the young, innocent, female role often found in pre-feminist plays. It comes from a Latin word for 'freeborn', with the implication that a freeborn person had more noble qualities than a slave. Hmm. Moving swiftly on, *ingenuous* is not to be confused with *disingenuous*, which means insincere while pretending to be sincere: 'It was *disingenuous* of him to claim that he hadn't known what the others were up to.' Nor is it the same as *ingenious*, which means clever, inventive, the work of a *genius*: 'She offered an *ingenious* solution to the problem.'

intrinsic

Inherent, fundamental to the nature of a thing: 'The value of the gold was less important than the necklace's *intrinsic* beauty.' From the Latin for 'inwards'.

invaluable

Not the opposite of *valuable*; here, the *in-* is an intensifier, so *invaluable* is so valuable that you can't put a price on it. Often used in a non-financial sense: 'His efforts made an *invaluable* contribution to our fundraising campaign.'

jejune

The original meaning of *jejune*, from a Latin word for 'fasting', was hungry or empty; from there it became insipid, lacking in taste – unsatisfying to the body. Then it was a short step to the more usual modern sense of unsatisfying to the mind and spirit – either boring, or naïve and unsophisticated, or both: 'His early diaries are *jejune* and self-obsessed, showing none of the political ACUMEN that made the later volumes so fascinating.'

leviathan

A huge aquatic creature mentioned in the Bible, *Leviathan* is also: the title of seventeenth-century philosopher Thomas Hobbes' 1651 study of society and government; one of a number of names for Isambard Kingdom Brunel's ship SS *Great Eastern*, by far the largest ever built at the time of her launch in 1858; and the name of a gigantic rollercoaster in Canada, a number of movies and a heavy-metal album loosely based on Herman Melville's classic novel about a whale, *Moby Dick*. So, a *leviathan* can be found in almost any field of endeavour, as long as it is vast and powerful.

linchpin

In the days when vehicles were supported by an axle-tree with a wheel at either end, a *linch-pin* was a pin passed through the end of the axle-tree to hold the wheel in place. An important part of the mechanism, in other words. A modern *linch-pin* or *linchpin*, therefore, is a component – human or otherwise – that is indispensable to the smooth running of any operation: 'The production department is the *linchpin* of the organization: we can't sell if we don't produce.' The word comes from Old English and has nothing to do with the hideous practice of *lynching* – hanging someone without trial – which is named after an eighteenth-century Virginian lawman who condoned it.

longevous

You may well be familiar with *longevity*, the quality of living or lasting a long time; this is the rarely used adjective derived from it. It can apply to individuals, races or things: Robert Louis Stevenson, extolling the pleasant feeling of what he called stupidity achieved by paddling a canoe, remarked that 'a man who has attained to this … begins to feel dignified and *longaevous* [*sic*] like a tree.'

majuscule

The opposite of *minuscule* in the typographic sense: in other words, a capital or 'upper case' letter. Unlike *minuscule*, which can be applied to anything tiny, not just a letter, *majuscule* is not generally used in a wider sense, which seems a shame. If you used it to mean 'huge', with the same enthusiasm that you would apply to HUMUNGOUS, it might catch on.

malleable

From the Latin for 'a hammer', this means able to be worked or hammered into shape without breaking – it's one of the defining characteristics of a metal. Using it figuratively, you might describe a person as having *a malleable disposition* if they always go along with what other people want to do.

manqué

A French word (pronounced roughly 'mong-kay') meaning 'failed' or 'not achieved', always placed after the noun it describes. *An actor manqué*, for example, tried to be an actor but didn't succeed; there's the teensiest hint that they compensate by showing off in other aspects of their life.

mantra

From the Sanskrit meaning 'instrument of thought', this is a sacred word or syllable in Hinduism and Buddhism (very often 'om'), repeated as an aid to meditation. In the secular sense, it means little more than a catchphrase or slogan: '"A place for everything and everything in its place" was my mother's *mantra*.'

mien

Pronounced 'mean', this is a person's look, bearing or manner, particularly if it indicates character or mood: *a noble mien* or *a dejected mien*. Oddly for such a short word, it seems to have been cobbled together from various sources, some English and some French.

mirific

Related to *miracle* and with the first syllable rhyming with 'eye', this means wonderful, working wonders or exciting amazement: 'It was a *mirific* achievement to get everyone together in the same place at the same time.' Not often used, but if you say it with the same rhythm as 'terrific', it has a zing to it.

moratorium

An agreed postponement of a decision, discussion or activity. This can either be something official, such as *an international moratorium on nuclear arms testing,* or more personal, like *a moratorium on discussing diet and exercise until the holidays are over.* From the Latin for 'a delay'.

myrmidon

A faithful follower, a henchman, with various shades of meaning: a *myrmidon* might simply be loyal but might also be a hanger-on, out for what they can get; or a mercenary soldier whose services can be bought and sold. From the name of a people of Ancient Greece who followed Achilles to the Trojan War.

nascent

Being born, starting to grow or develop. Often used of an idea or a business: 'Isaac Newton was a key figure in the *nascent* science of physics in the seventeenth century' or 'Henry Ford was quick to profit from the *nascent* interest in automobiles.' From the Latin for 'to be born', and therefore related to *native* and *natal.*

neologism

A new word or coinage, from Greek roots: 'Yuppy was a 1980s *neologism* that became established because it suited the mood of the times so well.'

neophyte

A beginner, a new recruit or a new convert to a religion. As with NEOLOGISM, *neo-* means new; *-phyte* is from the Greek for 'plant', so a *neophyte* is newly planted and inexperienced in whatever field it may be.

nomenclature

The assigning of names to things in a systematic way: 'Binomial *nomenclature* gives every living creature a two-part name, denoting its genus and species.' But the term can be used outside biology: in his 1858 novel *Doctor Thorne*, Anthony Trollope wrote of a dingy-looking pub called the Red Lion, noting that 'had it been called the brown lion, the *nomenclature* would have been more strictly correct.'

oneiric

To do with dreams, having a dreamlike quality: 'The *oneiric* cinematography added to the creepiness of the film.' From Greek and pronounced 'oh-nye-rick'.

panoply

Historically, all of a soldier's kit, a complete suit of armour; by extension any form of protection or, more usually, any impressive array: 'The herbaceous border displayed a glorious *panoply* of shapes, sizes and colours.' From the Greek for 'complete armour'.

paronomasia

Most people know what a pun is – a form of wordplay based on words that sound alike but have different meanings. Well, *pun* is far too simple a word for anyone studying rhetoric: they prefer *paronomasia*. To give a suitably literary example, the famous opening lines of Shakespeare's *Richard III*, 'Now is the winter of our discontent / Made glorious summer by this *sun* of York', pun on the fact that Edward IV was a 'son' of the House of York and that his symbol was a 'sun', which of course comes out more in 'summer'. As you can see, like most jokes, a *paronomasia* becomes less funny the moment you start trying to explain it.

paucity

A small quantity, not exactly a lack but certainly less than you might have hoped for: *a paucity of fruit* would make it difficult to make jam, while *a paucity of interesting company* makes for a dull party.

pedagogue

A teacher or tutor, particularly a strict and unlikeable one. What a *pedagogue* practises is *pedagogy* or *pedagoguery* and his approach may be described as *pedagogic*: fine words, all of them, but still expressing something negative: 'The teacher's *pedagogic* approach to chemistry took all the fun out of it: we were never allowed to set fire to anything.'

periphrasis

It's always pleasing when a great word can be defined by another great word, and here is a fine example: *periphrasis* means *circumlocution*. The former is Greek in origin, the latter is Latin, but they both come from words meaning 'talking around' – in other words, failing to get to the point, expressing something in lots of words when one or two would do. Enough said?

peroration

The end of an *oration*, particularly an impressive, rousing one: 'While the main part of the speech dealt with economic policy, the *peroration* was a passionate plea for religious tolerance.'

phalanx

Ancient Greek infantrymen formed a *phalanx* by lining up closely in a rectangle and forming an impenetrable barrier with their shields and spears. If you don't happen to be in the Ancient Greek infantry, you might form *a phalanx of support* for a cause, in order to present a united front. To justify being called a phalanx there has to be quite a number of you, and you need to be close-knit and organized. The plural may be *phalanxes* or *phalanges*; the latter is the name given to the bones of the fingers and toes, which are also close to each other and arranged in an orderly fashion.

plenipotentiary

Something beginning with *pleni-* is likely to mean full; *potentiary* is related to *potent*, to do with power. So, a *plenipotentiary* is full of power – the power to represent their country as an ambassador, for example, or to conduct business on behalf of a company. Such a person could also be said to have *plenipotentiary powers*. See also PLENARY.

quasi

Latin for 'as if', 'almost' and used in English before a noun or an adjective to indicate attempting to be or to copy something without quite succeeding. A *quasi-revolution* causes some upheaval, but doesn't actually overthrow a government; *quasi soul music* isn't soulful enough to be called soul; *quasi-intellectuals* aren't as bright or as well read as they would have you believe.

ramification

Something that spreads out like branches (Latin *ramus*), usually a consequence that makes things more complicated: 'The fact that there was no written contract led to all sorts of *ramifications* about who was responsible for what.'

rapprochement

A French word meaning 'bringing closer together', especially after a disagreement; a reconciliation. Often used in the context of international relations – 'The election of a more liberal leader led to a *rapprochement* with the West' – but can also be more personal – 'The arrival of a baby niece brought a *rapprochement* between the two sisters, who had hardly spoken for years.'

recidivist

The SEPULCHRAL voice at the start of the classic 1970s television comedy *Porridge* intones, 'Norman Stanley Fletcher ... you are an habitual criminal'; had the writers been striving for a different tone the line could easily have been 'You are a *recidivist*', because it means someone who relapses into crime, a frequent reoffender. It can also be an adjective – you could have *recidivist tendencies* – and it comes from the Latin for 'to fall'. The verb *to recidivate* is less commonly used, but exists should you happen to need it.

refractory

From a Latin word meaning 'broken', this has various technical meanings in science and medicine, but in non-scientific use means obstinate or uncontrollable. It first appears in Shakespeare's *Troilus and Cressida*, when the Trojan hero Hector speaks of civilized countries having laws 'to curb those raging appetites that are most disobedient and *refractory*'.

Rubicon

The Rubicon was and is a river in northern Italy, just inland from Rimini; in 49 BC it marked the boundary between Cisalpine Gaul and Italia. Most of us think of Gaul as being synonymous with modern France, but *cisalpine* means 'on this side of the Alps' (from the Roman point of view, i.e. the southern side) and that region extended well into modern Italy. Julius Caesar, on his way back from wars in Gaul, crossed the Rubicon with an army at his back – an action which was strictly against the law and effectively meant he was declaring war on the establishment at Rome. *To cross the Rubicon*, therefore, means to commit yourself to a course of action, to do something that cannot be undone; *a Rubicon* is a point of no return.

sartorial

Sartor is Latin for 'a tailor', so *sartorial* refers – often satirically – to the way a person is dressed. The most commonly used phrase is probably *sartorial elegance*, although Robert Galbraith's 2013 novel *The Cuckoo's Calling* describes the UNKEMPT detective Cormoran Strike as attempting 'to counter his visitor's *sartorial* superiority by projecting the air of a man too busy to worry about laundry'.

saturnine

Relating to the planet *Saturn,* which in astrology made those born under its influence either gloomy and antisocial, or dark and stern in appearance, or both. Oddly, the Roman god Saturn is associated with plenty, wealth and celebration: the annual *Saturnalia* festival was an occasion for uninhibited merrymaking.

simulacrum

From the Latin for 'likeness' and related to *similar* and *simulate,* this is a representation of someone or something, usually a vague or superficial likeness, lacking in substance: 'The smart clothes produced the *simulacrum* of a successful businessman, but underneath he was still a dodgy wheeler-dealer.'

trope

From Ancient Greek and Latin words for 'to turn', this means a word or expression used in a figurative sense (of which there are plenty of examples scattered throughout this book); it can also refer to an extended metaphor, as in the theme of a book, play or the like: 'The author used the *trope* of alienated teenagers to discuss the position of disadvantaged people in all areas of society.'

vernacular

The indigenous language of a country or a district. This isn't the same as a dialect, which differs from the standard version of its own language; rather, the *vernacular* is distinct from the language of a conquering people or a language – English, perhaps, or Mandarin – that is not the native tongue but is widely used in education or business. When the *vernacular* replaced Latin as the language of the Roman Catholic Mass in the mid-1960s, this meant that subsequent Masses were held in English in England, in French in France, and so on. The word may also be an adjective, as in *the vernacular architecture* of people's houses, as opposed to the imported neo-classical style of civic buildings. More loosely, it can be applied to slang, jargon and even swearing: 'If you don't like it, to use the *vernacular*, you can damn well lump it.'

vouchsafe

To grant, frequently in a condescending way and used negatively: 'She *vouchsafed* no reply to my letter.' Related to *vouch for*, meaning to give an assurance about someone, but more pompous than that.

CHAPTER THREE

Words That Relieve Your Feelings

Sometimes you have to let rip. When disasters happen, when you are spoiling for a fight or when you want to tear someone's character to shreds behind their back, it's good to have words that match your mood.

acidulous

Sour, acid-like – literally in taste, figuratively in speech or attitude. In the literal sense, it needn't be unpleasant: the addition of lemon juice might give a sauce an agreeably *acidulous* tang. But with people, it is less likely to be nice: 'His mother's *acidulous* remarks about his cooking made him regret inviting her to lunch.'

acquisitive

Greedy, longing to *acquire* things, usually material possessions (*acquisitions*) or money. Not an attractive characteristic, though it's not alone in that: the twentieth-century American journalist Walter Lippmann covered quite a few when he observed that 'Corrupt, stupid, grasping functionaries will make at least as big a muddle of socialism as stupid, selfish and *acquisitive* employers can make of capitalism.'

altercation

A heated dispute, an argument: 'Raised voices and the sound of broken crockery suggested that an *altercation* was going on next door.'

animosity

From a neutral Latin word *animus* meaning 'spirit', this has over the years acquired the sense of ill feeling, hostility or resentment: 'I have no *animosity* towards relations in general; I just don't happen to like my own.'

antipathy

Dislike, hostility, a lack of fellow feeling – the opposite of *sympathy*: 'There is a long-standing *antipathy* between my family and his, and I have never had anything to do with them.'

apoplectic

Suffering from *apoplexy,* a sudden loss of consciousness caused by a rupture of a blood vessel in the brain, or from symptoms similar to those of apoplexy. Loosely, this generally means turning red in the face from furious anger: 'He was *apoplectic* with rage; he couldn't speak and looked as if he might burst out of his jacket.'

apostate

Someone who indulges in *apostasy*, from the Greek for 'standing apart from'. It means deserting a cause, renouncing your religious or political beliefs and possibly going over to the other side. See also TERGIVERSATE.

arbitrary

An *arbiter* is a judge, a referee, one who has the last word: 'The Human Resources Director is the final *arbiter* in disputes between members of staff.' It's to be hoped that such a person makes a rational decision. But the related adjective *arbitrary* suggests the opposite: *an arbitrary decision* is based on the prejudices of the person making it or on the whim of a moment: 'Sometimes she insists on

having her main meal at midday, sometimes in the evening.
It seems completely *arbitrary* to me.'

arriviste

A French word, related to *arrive* and meaning 'one who
has recently arrived on the social scene': similar to a
parvenu and likely to be *nouveau riche* as well. In addition
to lacking breeding and gentility, *arrivistes* are ruthless in
their efforts to improve their social status. All things that
aristocrats traditionally disapprove of.

Babbitt

In 1930, Sinclair Lewis became the first American to
receive the Nobel Prize in Literature, largely thanks to his
1922 novel, *Babbitt*. The book was successful enough for
the name of its protagonist, George F. Babbitt, to pass into
the language as the archetype of a mediocre, complacent,
middle-class man. It's not often used any more, but if you
say it impatiently enough people will get the idea.

besmirch

To soil, smear, make dirty or, metaphorically, to tarnish or
damage (as with a reputation). Oddly, it seems to come from
an Old French word meaning 'to torture with hot metal', but
in modern use you are more likely to be *besmirched* with
mud or by slander. You can also be *smirched*, but the *be-*
prefix (meaning around, on all sides, as in *beset* or *bedazzle*)
makes it feel more intense. Or muddier.

calamity

A disaster, but not just any disaster: this is an extra specially catastrophic one. In Shakespeare's *Romeo and Juliet*, after Mercutio and Tybalt have been killed, Friar Lawrence says to Romeo:

Affliction is enamour'd of thy parts,
And thou art wedded to calamity.

In other words, sorrow and disaster follow wherever Romeo goes – which, of course, becomes more and more true as the play progresses.

cataclysm

Another type of disaster, the really thorough kind that destroys whatever has gone before. It applied initially to the Biblical Flood, which covered the Earth after forty days and forty nights of rain, but has latterly been extended to cover social and political disasters, too: 'The *cataclysm* of the French Revolution swept away the monarchy and introduced the First Republic.'

catatonic

In a state of *catatonia*, characterized by muscular rigidity and stupor, a condition sometimes associated with schizophrenia. In casual use, it means immobile and unresponsive, possibly because you are drunk to the point of near-unconsciousness.

contumacious

A grand word for obstinate, determined to resist authority.
The related noun *contumacy* also has the specific meaning
of refusing to appear in court or to comply with a court
order; it is not to be confused with *contumely*, which means
insulting language or behaviour. Hamlet's 'To be, or not
to be' soliloquy mentions 'the proud man's *contumely*'
as one of the problems of life he wouldn't have to deal
with if he decided to end it all. Work *contumely* into your
conversation, therefore, and you will be in distinguished
(if potentially suicidal) company.

craven

Of obscure origin and rather old-fashioned, but a powerful
alternative to coward or cowardly. When the nineteenth-
century historian Lord Macaulay, writing about the end
of James II's inglorious reign, observed that in the King's
mind 'all other feelings had given place to a *craven* fear for
his life', it was a strong thing to say.

demean

To lower your standards, to behave in a way you find
shameful; often used in the negative: 'I refuse to *demean*
myself by entering into that argument.' It's related to *mean*
in the sense of inferior or lowly. A different, rarely used
verb *to demean* comes from words meaning to drive or
lead and means to behave in a certain way; this is related to
demeanour, signifying bearing or appearance.

despotic

In Ancient Greece, a *despot* was originally a master or lord ruling over a household, but as that household would have included slaves over whom he had absolute power, the word took on that connotation – an absolute ruler and, by extension, a tyrannical, oppressive one. *Despotic*, therefore, means overbearingly powerful, ruling cruelly and without any controls being put on you. You don't have to be in charge of a kingdom, though: a bossy head teacher or office manager could rule their own little empire *despotically*. *Tyrannical* means much the same thing; if you were looking to distinguish the two, you could say that the *tyrant* seized power while the *despot* acquired theirs legitimately. But that is a nit-picking distinction: once they are in power there is little to choose between them.

detriment

Harm, disadvantage: 'He worked far too hard, to the *detriment* of his health and his marriage.' From a Latin word meaning 'to wear away', so there is an element of ATTRITION involved: *detriment* tends not to happen overnight.

diabolical

Similar to MEPHISTOPHELEAN, but easier to spell and to pronounce, this means to do with the Devil and all his works, evil, fiendish: 'They concocted a *diabolical* plot to cheat their cousin out of his inheritance.' *Diabolical* is also used as an intensifier, along the lines of *bloody* or *damned*, though it's not a swear word. It's often found in the expression *a diabolical liberty*, meaning something that you think is unfair and that you are thoroughly aggrieved about.

disdainful

Showing or feeling *disdain* – scorn, a combination of superiority and dislike: 'She didn't answer my question, just gave me a *disdainful* glance and turned away.' *Disdain* can also be a verb: 'She *disdained* to answer my question.' From an Old French word meaning 'to reject as unworthy', which is exactly what a *disdainful* person does.

dissolute

Debauched, given to loose behaviour: the historian Thomas M. Lindsay, writing about the Protestant Reformation in sixteenth-century Europe, noted that 'the rule of *dissolute* bishops and the example of a turbulent and immoral clergy had poisoned the morals of the city' (Geneva, in case it sounds like a place you'd like to visit). It's related to *dissolve*, and the noun *dissolution* normally means something to do with dissolving; if you wanted a noun to apply to the Genevan bishops, it would be *dissoluteness*.

dyspeptic

Suffering from *dyspepsia*, having difficulty with your digestion. A symptom of the disease is a tendency to low spirits and/or irritability, so *dyspeptic* can mean gloomy, depressed or bad-tempered, whether or not you can blame these things on digestive troubles.

encumbrance

A hindrance or burden, something that is *cumbersome*, in either a literal or a figurative sense: 'The presence of a chaperone was something of an *encumbrance* to courtship.'

erratic

'*To err* is human,' they say, but *to err* is also to make a mistake, to wander from the straight and narrow, to go astray. *Erratic* derives from this and means prone to wandering, having no fixed course: 'He pursued an *erratic* course home from the pub.' It can also mean unreliable: 'My *erratic* uncle may or may not turn up at my birthday party.' From the same Latin root comes *errant*, as in the medieval *knight errant*, who wandered from place to place in search of adventure. In modern use, *errant* is more disapproving than *erratic*: *erratic behaviour* is no more than unpredictable; *errant behaviour* deviates from accepted standards.

erroneous

Also derived from the Latin for 'to wander or err' (see ERRATIC), this means containing *errors*. So something *erroneous* is incorrect, misguided, just plain wrong: 'I was under the *erroneous* impression that my contribution would be welcome.'

excrescence

In his 1933 memoir *Down and Out in Paris and London*, George Orwell wrote about the curious attitude of society towards tramps, of which there were many thousands in England at the time: 'It is taken for granted that a beggar does not "earn" his living, as a bricklayer or a literary critic "earns" his. He is a mere social *excrescence*, tolerated because we live in a humane age, but essentially despicable.'

Literally, an *excrescence* is anything that grows outwards – a wart on a human finger, for example, or the swellings on some trees known as galls. But it's usually unhealthy, or at least undesirable – and that's the implication in the Orwell quote, too.

execrable

Strictly speaking involving a curse or *execration*, this can be used loosely to mean appalling or very bad: 'He may be handsome, but he has *execrable* taste in clothes.'

exorbitant

Literally off the right track, out of *orbit*, but generally used to mean excessive, especially with reference to money – 'The banks charge an *exorbitant* rate of interest' – or power – 'He had an *exorbitant* influence on the careers of his former students.' A lot, in other words, but in a bad way.

expostulate

To protest against something, but in a reasonable manner, when trying to dissuade someone from doing something: 'He *expostulated* against my holiday plans, saying he would be bored stiff lying on a beach for a week.' Strictly speaking, you can't lose your temper when you are expostulating, however tempted you may be. It comes from a Latin word meaning 'to assert or claim', which also gives us *to postulate*, to put forward a theory.

fabrication

The act of *fabricating* – constructing, manufacturing in a way that requires skill – or the result of it. Originally, therefore, *fabrication* was the creating of a finished product; now it's more likely to be a product of the imagination, a lie or a fake: 'The confession he made to the police was pure *fabrication*.'

facetious

Frivolous, facile, a little foolish: inappropriately light-hearted. You could be a naturally *facetious person*, refusing to take life seriously, or you could just make *a facetious remark* at a time when a bit of sympathy might have gone down better. See also FLIPPANT and, for a different reason, ABSTEMIOUS.

foolhardy

A combination of *foolish* and *hardy* (or perhaps *hardi*, the French for 'bold'), this means stupidly adventurous, not stopping to think before doing something: 'Walking so close to the cliff edge wasn't brave, it was downright *foolhardy*.'

fustian

An old-fashioned word due for a revival. Originally a sort of coarse cloth, it came to be used to mean high-flown language or speech, unnecessary ranting. Try it and you'll find you can say it with a satisfactory amount of venom: 'Don't you talk *fustian* to me!'

heinous

Appalling, dreadful, wicked, vicious: *heinous deeds*, *a heinous crime*, *a heinous abuse of power* – they're all about as bad as they can be. From the French for 'hate', with the first syllable rhyming with 'pain'.

imprecation

A curse, calling down evil on someone's head; more loosely, any form of swearing. It's a useful word when you don't want to quote something offensive verbatim. The 1945 novel *Murder by Matchlight* by E. C. R. Lorac tells us that a character 'sat still and swore, vigorously and persistently, uttering many strange colourful *imprecations*' – a turn of phrase that clearly indicated immoderate language without shocking Ms Lorac's readers.

incendiary

Setting on fire, as in *an incendiary bomb*, which bursts into flame when it hits its target. Also used for something that will inflame feelings without actually setting fire to them: 'His *incendiary* language was bound to lead to trouble' or 'It was an *incendiary* situation: the crowd was ready to run riot.' From the Latin for 'a fire', but not the kind that burns gently in the fireplace.

ingrate

An *ungrateful* person. It may not sound much, but try yelling, 'You ... you ... you *ingrate!*' when you're really cross with someone for taking you for granted. Chances are you'll feel better.

ingratiate

To work your way into someone's good *graces*, to do things deliberately to please them or gain their favour: 'He *ingratiated* himself with the boss by making sure her coffee was always waiting for her when she came in.'

inveigh

Pronounced 'in-vay', this is to speak violently, usually against something: 'He *inveighed* against declining standards in journalism.' From the Latin meaning 'to be carried into and thence to assault', it's related to *invective*, the violent language you might use if you were *inveighing* against someone. *Invective* doesn't usually involve swearing – it's more likely to be sarcastic or bitter, but it is definitely fierce.

malinger

To pretend to be ill – or more ill than you really are – in order to get out of work or to WANGLE some benefit: 'The army doctor complained that his patients were all *malingerers*, hoping to be sent home.' Its origins aren't clear, but it may be a combination of the French *mal*, meaning 'bad or ill', and *linger*, to lag behind, not wanting to leave somewhere.

mountebank

From the Italian for 'to climb on a bench', this was originally a vendor of quack medicines (who would have done business by standing on a raised platform in the marketplace in order to attract attention); then it came to be a charlatan or fraud in any field of endeavour, especially someone who is out to take money from you or to build their own reputation on false grounds. A slightly old-fashioned word that still has its uses.

opportunist

One who grabs an *opportunity* and turns it to their advantage. This can be an animal – 'Foxes are *opportunist* feeders, raiding rubbish bins and eating whatever they find there' – or a person – 'He was the complete *opportunist*, turning up at the scene of any disaster in the hope that he would be photographed looking compassionate.'

ostracize

To exclude someone from a group or society. From the Greek for a broken piece of pottery which was used to mark a vote on whether or not to send someone into temporary exile. Modern ostracism doesn't necessarily involve making someone leave town; it's more cold-shouldering them as a sign of disapproval: 'He was *ostracized* at work after refusing to join the union.'

overweening

Arrogant, immoderate, extravagant: from an Old English word meaning 'to think or imagine', with *over* obviously indicating doing it to excess: 'I was flabbergasted by what he said: I couldn't believe the *overweening* nerve of the man.'

pabulum

A word with a chequered career, this comes from the Latin for 'to feed' (it's related to *pasture*) and started out as a neutral term for any sort of nourishment taken in by a plant or animal. Then it rose to signify something that nourishes the soul or spirit, 'food for thought', and has now sunk again to meaning bland, undemanding writing or entertainment, such as *a pabulum of cheap romance.* Longer and more pretentious than *pap*, but serving the same purpose.

paltry

Very small (particularly of a sum of money), insignificant
– and insultingly so: 'He offered me a *paltry* ten dollars; it's
worth three times that.' From a Germanic word meaning
'ragged'.

pernicious

Destructive, malevolent: *pernicious diseases* are potentially
fatal and *pernicious influences* – on society or on a person's
character, perhaps – are non-life-threatening but harmful.
Although the word comes from a Latin term for 'death by
violence', nowadays something *pernicious* is likely to be
slow-moving but far-reaching, spreading its evil influence
gradually: 'The *pernicious* effect of fake news makes it
difficult to know what to believe.'

pestiferous

Plague-bearing, but more generally used in a figurative
sense meaning harmful: 'A *pestiferous* tendency to ignore
the needs of the underprivileged.'

pettish

Childishly bad-tempered, sulky or quick to take the *pet* in
the old-fashioned sense of taking offence: 'He was very
pettish on anyone else's birthday – he hated not being the
centre of attention.'

philanderer

Its Greek origins indicate that this word began as 'a lover of men', but it's used in English to mean a lover (for want of a better word) of women: an unfaithful one, who flits from one woman to another, flirting and probably seducing as he goes. It's often used by headline-writers to describe a public figure – a politician, an actor, the usual – who has been caught having an affair. But if you aspire to be a full-scale *philanderer*, one or two affairs won't do: you have to make a habit of it. Like most of the words in this chapter, it isn't a compliment.

philodox

Words beginning with *phil-* tend to indicate a love of something (see PHILANDERER, but there's also *philosophy*, a love of knowledge or wisdom, and *Philadelphia*, the City of Brotherly Love); the *-dox* in *philodox* means opinion and is also found in *orthodox*, following accepted opinion or practice. A *philodox*, therefore, is a lover of opinions – their own opinions. They are dogmatic, argumentative, dictatorial and probably bigoted as well. The *OED* gives this great citation from a 1958 issue of the Berkshire (Massachusetts) *Eagle*: 'One grows weary of the sickening sophomoric twaddle of our local pansophic *philodox*.' To translate: British English would probably say *undergraduate* rather than *sophomoric;* TWADDLE is pompous nonsense; *pansophic* describes a know-it-all. Put them all together and you have a beautiful put-down.

poltroon

If ever you feel that describing someone as a wretched, snivelling coward isn't strong enough, try this. The *OED* describes its use as 'now chiefly archaic or humorous', but you can still get a lot of venom into it. Throwing in CRAVEN or *lily-livered* as well makes it even better. From a Middle French word meaning 'cowardly, lazy, good-for-nothing...' you get the idea.

pontificate

Originally, and with no suggestion of disapproval, this meant to behave like the *pontiff* or Pope, to officiate at a solemn Mass. Its modern meaning is less respectful: *to pontificate* is to speak in a pompous or dogmatic manner, laying down the law about something you may know little about. It needn't have any connection with religion: 'She once did a week's internship at the BBC and now she *pontificates* about camera angles and lighting whenever we turn on the television.'

poseur

The French word for 'poser', someone who adopts attitudes or opinions in order to impress others: 'He's such a *poseur* that he won't read anything but the latest literary fiction.' Strictly speaking the feminine is *poseuse*, but only the most dedicated *poseur* would make the distinction.

precocious

Ahead of the normal stage of development, smarter than might be expected for someone your age. Most frequently used of a child and all too often in phrases such as *precocious brat*: one who is too clever by half and not afraid to show it. It's from the Latin for 'ripening early', and has a more technical sense with reference to plants or fruits that flower or ripen early in the season.

preposterous

Originally, out of position or order, with the thing that should have been *pre* (before) placed *post* (after). Now used more loosely to mean ridiculous or outrageous or both: 'You can't be serious – that is a *preposterous* suggestion!' Guides to good writing always say you should use exclamation marks sparingly, but something that is preposterous deserves one.

puerile

Childish (from the Latin *puer*, meaning 'a boy'), but in an unpleasant, immature, old-enough-to-know-better sort of way. Only an adult can be *puerile* and, while playing childish jokes may be amusing, being *puerile* is not.

putrid

Rotten – either literally decomposing or morally corrupt. You could come across *the putrid corpse of a dead rabbit* or deplore *the putrid influence of online bullying.* Either way, it stinks.

recriminatory

Related to *crime* and *incriminate*, this means involving *recriminations*, which are strictly speaking counter-accusations against someone who has accused you of something. The word can also be used more loosely to describe criticisms or reproaches of any kind: 'In the months before we finally separated, there was always a *recriminatory* tone to our conversation.'

sanctimonious

Affectedly pious, condescendingly virtuous. From the Latin word for 'holy', but much less approving than that sounds. Politicians – in the UK House of Commons, at least – are fond of accusing each other of *sanctimonious humbug*, *sanctimonious self-congratulation*, *sanctimonious hypocrisy* and even, once, in a clear case of unparliamentary language, *sanctimonious claptrap*.

scabrous

Related to the unpleasant skin condition *scabies* (and pronounced with a long 'a' – as in 'skate' rather than 'scab'), this means literally rough or scaly, but figuratively indelicate, improper: *scabrous humour*, *scabrous sex scenes*. Not SALACIOUS or fun, just grubby.

sciolism

With the first syllable pronounced 'sigh', this is superficial knowledge, especially if the *sciolist* is pretending to be an expert. From the Latin for 'to know' and therefore related to *science,* it's not often used but was a favourite insult of nineteenth-century men of letters. The novelist Charles Kingsley wrote of 'the tendency to shallow and conceited *sciolism*, engendered by hearing popular lectures on all manner of subjects' and the politician William Gladstone believed that specialism, though not without its faults, was 'to be preferred to pretentious and flaunting *sciolism*'.

squalor

If you've spent any time in *squalor* (or in *squalid surroundings*), you'll almost certainly want to have a shower and change your clothes: it means disgustingly dirty and smelly, often as a result of poverty and neglect. The Latin root means 'to be stiff with dirt', which gives you an idea of how unpleasant it is. Many people in Dickensian London *lived in squalor* through no fault of their own; you might also find *a scene of squalor* if you came home early before the kids had had time to clear up after a party.

temerity

Rashness; going a step beyond boldness and towards barefaced cheek: 'He had the *temerity* to deny that he had been smoking when he positively reeked of tobacco.'

tergiversate

Literally to turn one's back, but used in the sense of deserting one's party, one's friends or indeed one's principles. Like the similar APOSTATE, it's a bad thing, as can be seen in this scathing line from the nineteenth-century Scottish writer John Wilson: '"I am liberal in my politics," says some twenty-times *tergiversated* turn-coat.'

trumpery
Connected with the French *tromper*, 'to deceive', this refers to something that may be superficially attractive but is basically worthless. It can be a noun or an adjective: a necklace made of glass rather than diamonds could be described as *trumpery* or as a piece of *trumpery jewellery*. It's a word that can be spoken with a good deal of contempt, too: in the 1926 novel *Lolly Willowes* by Sylvia Townsend Warner, the middle-aged Lolly, fed up with her brother's list of reasons why she shouldn't set up house on her own, utters the splendid words, 'Have done with your *trumpery* red herrings!' That's an expression we could all adopt for use in moments of exasperation.

unconscionable
Having no *conscience* or scruples, often in expressions such as *an unconscionable liar* or *an unconscionable rogue*: 'He is such an *unconscionable* liar, I don't think it would ever occur to him to tell the truth.'

unmitigated
If you failed to complete an assignment because you were ill, these might be described as *mitigating circumstances*

– circumstances that make the offence less serious (*mitigating* comes from the Latin word for 'mild'). Something that is *unmitigated*, therefore, is as severe and absolute as it can be: *an unmitigated tragedy* is a complete and utter tragedy; *an unmitigated villain* or *an unmitigated hypocrite* is a prime example of the type.
See also EXTENUATE.

vainglory

Glory that is *vain;* that is, empty boasting, unjustified pride in one's supposed achievements. When the sixteenth-century Duke of Somerset, Lord Protector of England during the reign of his nephew Edward VI, fell from grace, the teenage King recorded in his diary that the charges against his uncle included 'ambition, *vainglory* … enriching himself of my treasure, following his own opinion, and doing all by his own authority'. In 1552, that ensured you had your head cut off; even today it could lead you into trouble.

varlet

A knave, a rogue. Related to *valet*, it originally meant any male servant in a menial position, even a well-behaved and virtuous one, but then developed into a term of disapproval and contempt. Shakespeare uses it in both senses but when, in *King Lear*, one character describes another as 'a brazen-faced *varlet*' and, in *Measure for Measure*, in the course of a heated dispute someone shouts, '*Varlet*, thou liest; thou liest, wicked *varlet*', it's clear that something other than an obedient servant is meant.

vaunt

To show off, to display ostentatiously – related to *vanity*.
You can *vaunt your engagement ring* or *vaunt your newly
acquired knowledge*; you can also *vaunt that you won every
game*, but it's all pretty boastful and won't win you friends.

verbiage

The use of too many words, especially meaningless ones
that attempt to obscure the point (or to disguise the
fact that there isn't a point). The Austrian psychoanalyst
Wilhelm Reich put it beautifully when he said:

> *In many cases, the function of speech has deteriorated to
> such a degree that the words express nothing whatever
> … Endless numbers of speeches, publications, political
> debates do not have the function of getting at the root
> of important questions of life but of drowning them in
> verbiage.*

He was writing in 1933, but some things don't change.

wastrel

A ne'er-do-well, a *wasteful*, spendthrift, unreliable person.
Rather old-fashioned, but can be spoken with a pleasing
amount of invective: 'That *wastrel*? I wouldn't give him the
time of day, never mind lend him money.'

CHAPTER FOUR

Words That Make You Laugh

If some words sound beautiful and others sound clever, there are those whose existence simply cheers you up.

bamboozle

To cheat, mislead or confuse: 'He's trying to *bamboozle* me with statistics, but I'm sure he doesn't know what he's doing.' Suitably, the word's origins are unclear.

bandy

If you are *bandy* or *bandy-legged*, your legs curve outwards at the knees, but the verb *to bandy* means to toss something back and forth; it may come from an Old French tennis term. You can *bandy words* with someone – disagree with them, listen to their counter-argument and disagree with that, too; or you can *bandy their name about*, spreading rumours about them and bringing them into disrepute.

blatherskite

Also spelled *bletherskate*, this is a colloquial Scots word that became popular in the USA at the time of the War of Independence and means someone who talks a lot of nonsense. *To blether* or *to blather* means to talk in this way. To be clear, we are referring to both quantity and lack of quality here: a blatherskite talks *a lot*, as well as saying nothing worth listening to. A variation on this is *blither* – often found in the adjectival form *blithering*, which means little more than 'complete and utter'. If you describe someone as *a blithering idiot*, you probably think that they have just done something very idiotic indeed.

boggle

Often in humorous expressions such as *the mind boggles* or *the imagination boggles*, this is to be amazed, confused and rather shocked all at the same time: 'He tells me he's going to wear shorts and a Hawaiian shirt to the awards ceremony – the mind *boggles*.' You can also *boggle at* something, meaning to hesitate to do something or object to it because it is going too far. It's frequently used in the negative: 'He wouldn't *boggle* at borrowing money from you; he sponges off everyone.'

bootless

Useless, in vain. Nothing to do with boots, it comes from an Old English word meaning compensation. So, *a bootless errand* is not one that you ran in stockinged feet; it's one that there was no point in running, that achieved nothing and that brought no reward.

borborygmus

Also *borborygm*; not everyday words but glorious ones, meaning a rumbling in the gut or bowels. From a Greek word meaning the same thing. The author H. G. Wells obviously felt it deserved wider currency when he wrote, in the *Sunday Express* in 1927, 'elephant hunters say that they can tell the proximity of a herd by the *borborygmic* noises the poor brutes emit.' History does not record what the paper's readers made of that intriguing piece of information, but eleven years later the more serious *Times* was describing the intestinal noises made by Arabian camels in the same way.

caboodle

Often in the expressions *the whole caboodle* or *the whole kit and caboodle*, this is a colloquial term for the whole lot, everything but the kitchen sink. One of the meanings of *kit* is just that: a full set or collection of people or things; and *boodle* comes from a Dutch word for 'a person's entire property'. So why *kit and caboodle* rather than *kit and boodle*? Well, the latter is sometimes used (largely in the USA), but phrasemakers do love alliteration. It's the same principle as lay behind the idea of being *as fit as a fiddle* or *as right as rain* – someone somewhere presumably just thought that *kit and caboodle* made a satisfactory phrase.

cahoots

Usually *to be in cahoots* with someone, to be in league with them. Originally an innocent enough colloquial American term for a partnership, it's acquired the suggestion that you are up to no good: 'They were in *cahoots* with the magistrate to see that they got off with a warning.' Possibly from a French word meaning 'a cabin', because that was where you had your secret conferences.

caterwaul

As perfect a word for 'to make an appalling noise' as the English language has to offer. For once, it can be taken at face value: it *was* originally to do with *cats*, specifically the noise they make at mating time. But it can also be applied to humans, whether mating or not: singing noisily and out of tune in the middle of the night could be described as *caterwauling*, particularly by a neighbour who was trying to sleep.

cavort

To prance or CAPER, to play joyfully and perhaps a little naughtily or sexily. There's a term in dressage, *curvet*, which means a low leap with all four feet (the horse's feet, obviously) off the ground, and it's possible that *cavort* is a corruption of this.

chicanery

Trickery, deception, quibbling or sharp practice, especially in matters of law: 'He languished in prison while the prosecution wasted time in *chicaneries*.' From the same French word that gives us *chicane*, meaning either a sharp bend on a motor-racing circuit or a way of narrowing lanes on a motorway, which are both designed to force drivers to slow down.

concatenation

From the Latin for 'chain' and often appearing in the expression *a concatenation of circumstances*: a chain of closely linked events in which one thing leads inevitably but perhaps unexpectedly to another.

diablerie

Originally something connected with the Devil (see
DIABOLICAL) – an evil deed, witchcraft or a representative
of the Devil. The meaning then softened into something
more like *devil-may-care* – denoting mischief and
recklessness rather than evil. In P. G. Wodehouse's 1963
novel *Stiff Upper Lip, Jeeves*, the narrator Bertie Wooster
says of a dashing new hat that 'it unquestionably lent a
diablerie to my appearance, and mine is an appearance
that needs all the *diablerie* it can get.' It's a French word,
so you need to say it with *élan* or *panache* – that is, with a
touch of style.

finagle

Originally American and a near-synonym of WANGLE: to use
devious means to achieve your own ends. Possibly from an
Old English dialect word meaning to cheat.

flibbertigibbet

An unreliable, flighty, irresponsible person, usually a
woman. She's probably a gossip, too, so don't trust her with
your money, your secrets or to turn up for work on time.
The word's origins are probably onomatopoeic:
it just *sounds* like mindless chatter. There's also an
adjective *flibberty-gibberty*, which surely deserves to be
more widely known.

flummery

Empty compliments, foolish, insincere talk, from a Welsh name for a jelly-like pudding. Perhaps the verbal sort of *flummery* wobbles and isn't very substantial, like its edible namesake?

flummox

To confuse, bewilder, BAMBOOZLE. In the *OED*'s first recorded use of the word, from Charles Dickens' *The Pickwick Papers* (1837), Sam Weller's father tells his son that, if Mr Pickwick doesn't provide an alibi in an impending court case, he'll be 'what the Italians call reg'larly *flummoxed*'. There's no suggestion anywhere else that this is an Italian word – it probably originates in English dialect, but that's not the sort of detail that would have bothered either of the Wellers.

gallivant

Gallivanting is the sort of wandering around that a gadabout or FLIBBERTIGIBBET does: going nowhere in particular but intent on having fun. You're unlikely to describe yourself as *gallivanting*, though: it's usually reserved for expressing disapproval of someone else's activities.

galumph

In Lewis Carroll's *Through the Looking-Glass* (published in 1871), Alice asks Humpty Dumpty to explain the meaning of the poem 'Jabberwocky', which baffled her a few chapters earlier. One of the words Humpty analyses is *slithy*: 'Well, "*slithy*" means "lithe and slimy". ... You see it's like a portmanteau – there are two meanings packed up into one word.'

As anyone who did any travelling in those days would have known, a portmanteau was a sort of suitcase, hinged so that it opened into two compartments, and 'Jabberwocky' contains a number of portmanteau words invented by Carroll. *Galumph* is a combination of *gallop* and *triumph*: the hero, having slain the monstrous Jabberwock,

> *... left it dead, and with its head*
> *He went galumphing back.*

Modern usage has drifted away from triumph to include an element of clumsiness and heavy-footedness: 'The way he *galumphed* across the floor made it hard to believe he'd ever had dancing lessons.'

Slithy, *mimsy* (*miserable* + *flimsy*) and *frabjous* (possibly *fair* + *joyous*) are three of Carroll's coinages that haven't really been adopted into the language; the other one that we do use is *chortle*, an expression of mirth that is a mixture of a *chuckle* and a *snort*.

guffaw

An echoic word (see the introduction) for a loud and hearty laugh, with perhaps just a hint of mockery of the person or thing that prompted it: 'He greeted the news with a disbelieving *guffaw*.'

humdinger

A slang term for someone or something excellent or outstanding, originating in the USA in the early twentieth century. Nobody is sure where and how it came into being, but it can be used to express approval of anything from a beautiful person to a fast car, a superb athlete to a sumptuous dessert: 'I tell you, she/he/it's a *humdinger*!'

humongous

Large – *very* large; a jokey slang word formed from a combination of *huge* and *monstrous*, with perhaps a bit of *tremendous* thrown in: 'After three *humongous* pieces of cake she somehow lost her enthusiasm for going to the gym.'

lambast

Either physically to beat or thrash or, more commonly, to give someone a tongue-lashing, to scold them violently. It's a combination of *to lam* and *to baste,* both of which mean to hit, and it's often used by headline-writers to convey an angry reaction to something: 'PM quotes Bible to *lambast* UNESCO decision on Hebron' was a 2017 headline in *The Times of Israel*, which went on to report that the Prime Minister was 'raging' over what UNESCO had done.

lampoon

To satirize, to send up, or, as a noun, the piece of writing, drawing or performance that does the *lampooning*.

Possibly from a French word meaning 'let us drink', suggesting that as we drink we'll become less discreet and say irreverent things about people in the public eye. Whether alcohol features or not, *lampoons* are meat and drink to political cartoonists and impressionists.

mordacious

From the Latin for 'to bite', this means biting in a figurative sense – sarcastic and cutting: 'As a theatre critic he was *mordacious* to the point of savagery, but in person he was surprisingly gentle.' Its near-synonym *mordant* is more commonly used, but *mordacious* has that extra hissing power that makes it satisfying to say out loud.

quibble

To nit-pick, to raise trivial objections that draw attention away from the main issue: 'He *quibbled* over the punctuation, when really it was the structure of the piece that needed attention.' Also a noun, meaning this sort of objection. Probably from the Latin *quibus*, meaning 'for whom' or 'by whom' – a word that occurred frequently in complicated legal documents in the days when these were written in Latin.

skinflint

To skin a flint – to take the skin off a hard piece of stone – is an old-fashioned expression that means to go to ridiculous lengths to save money; so a person who would do this, a mean, avaricious person, became a *skinflint.* The comparable *cheapskate* has nothing to do with skating in the ice- or roller- sense, but derives from *skate* as an old word for a worn-out horse. From there *skate* came to signify a mean and unpleasant person, so a *cheap skate* (originally two words) was not only unpleasant but also tight-fisted.

slurp
To drink noisily, or the noise made when *slurping.* It's often done with soup and is considered impolite, though bizarrely (given the Britishness of tea-drinking and the traditional British obsession with table manners) it's also the technical term for drinking tea (loudly) from a teaspoon during a tea-tasting.

snook
In the nineteenth-century, the expression *to take a sight* at a person meant 'to denote incredulity, or contempt for authority, by placing the thumb against the nose and closing all the fingers except the little one, which is agitated in token of derision'. (It's worth practising this before you try it on someone in authority, because it isn't easy to do.) A *snook* is the same action, and the word is used almost exclusively in the idiom *to cock a snook at*, to make this derisive gesture or to behave in a similarly mocking way: 'The article *cocked a snook* at the government's foreign policy.'

splendiferous

Abounding in splendour, an enthusiastic and jovial synonym for *splendid,* magnificent, lavish: you might have *a splendiferous dinner* on a special occasion or admire *a splendiferous sunrise* if you were up early enough to see it.

tatterdemalion

A little-known word that the *OED* defines with the aid of another delightful term that has fallen out of fashion: *ragamuffin.* Both mean a scruffily dressed person, the *tatterdemalion* being one who dresses in tatters while the *ragamuffin* is in rags. No one is sure where the *-muffin* part comes from – Ragamuffin was the name of a demon in the fourteenth-century poem *Piers Plowman*, so there may be connections with the Devil, but it's all a bit vague. As for *-demalion*, it seems to have been made up in order to turn the workaday adjective *tattered* into a rather feistier noun. Both words can also be used as adjectives, so you can have *ragamuffin clothes* or even *tatterdemalion scraps of knowledge.* Pretty scruffy, whichever version you choose.

tomfoolery

In medieval times, the name Tom was often used to indicate a generic example of a certain type of person: there are references to *Tom Tell-Truth* – an honest man – and *Tom All-Thumbs* – a clumsy one. So you also get *Tom Fool* or *Tomfool,* a stupid person or a clown or buffoon. It's the latter sense that is implied in *tomfoolery* – the sort of activity that a *tomfool* gets up to, frivolous behaviour or messing about: 'That's enough of your *tomfoolery* – you need to think seriously about getting a job.'

toothsome

Tasty, pleasant to the taste: *a toothsome risotto. Tooth* was in the past often used as a synonym for *taste*, as in having *a tooth for spicy food*, so *toothsome* is formed by analogy with *flavoursome*, *quarrelsome*, *tiresome* and many other words meaning 'containing that particular attribute'.

transmogrify

Of uncertain but probably jocular and/or uneducated origin, this means to change appearance, usually in a strange or grotesque way: 'Two drinks *transmogrified* him from an elegant and polite young man into a dishevelled and loud-mouthed ruffian.'

twaddle

One of those pleasurable words that can almost literally be spat off the tongue to convey contempt, this means silly, nonsensical talk or writing, particularly if it is wordy and affected. It's not clear where *twaddle* came from, but there is an earlier word, *twattle*, which is probably related to *tattle* and *title-tattle*, all of which are echoic (see the introduction).

If you think insults are more effective if they have only one brusque, dismissive syllable, there's always *tosh*, which means much the same thing.

vamoose

Adopted first into American English, from the Spanish *vamos* meaning 'let's go', this is to leave in a hurry, to scarper. There may be a suggestion of dishonesty – 'He *vamoosed* with all the cash we had taken that day' – or of irritation on the part of the person remaining behind – 'He was making a nuisance of himself, so I told him to *vamoose*.' *Skedaddle*, of obscure origin but popularized during the American Civil War, means much the same thing and is perhaps even more fun to say.

CHAPTER FIVE

Words That Are a Pleasure to Say

You can't beat ambrosia *and* mellifluous *for the way they flow gently off the tongue. Or can you ...? Here are a few words that enable you to wallow in the sheer joy of them.*

admonition
What you give when you *admonish* someone: a warning, caution or reprimand. A sensible hiker going off the beaten track would take heed of *admonitions* about carrying enough food, water and warm clothing.

adulation
Praise, but praise of the highest order, to the point of ridiculous flattery: a rock star might be overwhelmed by the *adulation of her fans.*

aggrandizement
Making *grander* – in status, power, wealth or whatever. Often seen in *self-aggrandizement*, which tells its own tale: 'The President's speech was supposed to be about spending more money on health care, but under the glitzy surface it was pure *self-aggrandizement.*'

allusion
The act of *alluding* to someone or something, making a reference to it: 'The scar on the forehead was an *allusion* to Harry Potter.' Not to be confused with *illusion*, which is a deceptive appearance – 'The shadow of the trees against the window gave the *illusion* of some monstrous being approaching the houses' – or a *delusion*, which is a false idea, often in the expression *delusions of grandeur*, thinking you are more important than you are.

ambrosia

In Classical mythology, long before anyone thought of putting rice pudding into a can, *ambrosia* was the food of the gods. As you can imagine, it tasted and smelled divine, so the word is now used to describe any supremely delicious food, drink or scent. A character in a London-based short story by Mollie Panter-Downes recalled a lavish lunch she had had before wartime rationing put an end to such things: 'They had had lobster salad at Scott's – an *ambrosial* lobster with thick mayonnaise, followed by raspberries and cream.' The original ambrosia conferred immortality on whoever consumed it; this lunch fell short of that, but did at least send the lady in question 'walking on air out into Piccadilly', which may be the next best thing.

audacious

Bold, daring: 'There was an *audacious* attempt to capture the enemy stronghold.' There's also the suggestion of cheekiness: *an audacious compliment* may be a little too SALACIOUS to pay to someone you've just met.

aura

This is the Latin for 'a breeze', but that meaning is rarely used in modern English. Instead, an *aura* is an emanation surrounding a person or thing, visible only to those with some sort of psychic power. Allegedly. It is also a sensation of noise or flashing lights, indicating the onset of an attack of epilepsy. And there is a figurative sense, according to which you may be surrounded by something intangible such as *an aura of authenticity* or *an aura of respectability*.

The suggestion here is that appearances are deceptive and that you aren't authentic or respectable at all.

bastion

Part of a fortification designed to facilitate defensive fire, and therefore anything strong and resistant to attack or change. Often in the expression *the last bastion of … hope, liberal democracy, good sense* or any other worthy quality that seems to be under threat.

beguiling

Charming, fascinating, but with a hint of slyness or deception – it's related to *guile*. So beware of someone who is *beguiling*: they're probably trying to trick you in some way.

bespoke

Usually of clothing, made to the customer's specification rather than bought off the peg; also used to describe the person who makes such clothes. Thus, you could order *a bespoke suit* from *a bespoke tailor*. More recently, other things have become *bespoke*, too: a PR agency might offer *bespoke services*, meaning it caters to a customer's particular requirements, rather than sending out the same old press release to the same old people; an IT or management consultant might also offer *bespoke solutions* to a client's problems; while the suppliers of *a bespoke vegetable box* would leave out the cauliflower if you said you didn't like it. It's related to the rather old-fashioned *bespeak*, meaning to order in advance, to reserve.

boisterous

No one is sure where it comes from, but this is an exuberant combination of noise, enthusiasm and unruly behaviour. At an early stage of Shakespeare's *Romeo and Juliet*, Romeo wonders, 'Is love a tender thing? It is too rough, too rude, too boisterous; and it pricks like a thorn.' But you don't have to be poetic with this word: you're more likely to find it in a context such as 'The young teacher found it hard to control her *boisterous* class.'

bravado

A combination of *braveness* and showing off; making a point of demonstrating how brave you are, often to cover up the fact that you are scared: 'He came on stage with a swagger, but it was pure *bravado* – he was terrified of speaking in public.'

capitulate

To yield, to surrender, particularly after holding out for a while, like a besieged fortress. Strictly, a *capitulation* involves negotiating terms, but in modern, non-military use it tends to mean giving in completely: 'The management *capitulated* to the workers' demands and awarded everyone an extra week's holiday.'

cascade

A waterfall or series of waterfalls; hence anything that falls and flows in the same way: 'Her veil was a *cascade* of lace.' It can also be a verb: 'The water *cascaded* over the rocks' or 'Her hair *cascaded* over her shoulders.' A French word that can be traced back to the Latin for 'to fall'.

celestial

Heavenly, either in the sense of divine or sublime, or of living in heaven. *Thy celestial home* was once a popular expression among Christian hymn-writers addressing God or the Holy Spirit, and Lord Byron speaks of St Peter sitting by *the celestial gate.* If you wanted to pay someone a slightly FLORID compliment, you could describe their eyes or perhaps their dress as being of a *celestial blue*. Or, on a more prosaic note, the word can also simply refer to the sky, particularly in the phrase *celestial bodies*, which means stars, planets and the like, visible from Earth but existing outside our atmosphere.

cerulean

If CELESTIAL doesn't do it for you and you're looking for a poetic word to describe the colour of the sky, this could be the one to go for. Pronounced 's'rule-ian', it means a deep blue – azure, if you like. It's a touch pretentious, so use it sparingly.

chanteuse

A French word, pronounced approximately 'shon-terz' or 'shon-tooz', meaning 'a female singer of popular songs', often found in a nightclub or cabaret. Why she should be given a French name when her male equivalent is likely to be a *crooner* is anyone's guess, but she typically has a husky voice and a melancholy repertoire, concentrating on heartbreak and men who have let her down.

charisma

From the Greek for 'grace', this was originally a Christian concept, a God-given power or talent. It's now moved out of the Church into the wider world and means a special personal quality that attracts, influences or inspires others: 'You may not approve of his opinions, but you can't deny he has *charisma*.' Someone with charisma is *charismatic,* as in 'He is such a *charismatic* actor – you can't take your eyes off him when he's on the screen.'

chatelaine

The mistress of a (grand) house or castle, related to *château*, the French for 'castle'. It's an old-fashioned word, obviously, as not many of us live in castles these days, but can still be used to describe a woman of authority and dignity. A *chatelaine* is also the name of the bunch of household keys that hung from such a woman's belt during medieval times, and of a smaller ornamental version of the same thing that women wore from the sixteenth to the nineteenth century.

concupiscence

Desire, longing, usually the sexual kind: the middle part of the word comes from the Latin for 'to desire' and is related to *Cupid* and *cupidity*. A nineteenth-century Christian tract maintained that marriage was designed as *a remedy against concupiscence* – in other words, apparently, it stopped you from lusting after anyone but your spouse. Hmm. Pronounced 'con-queue-pi-sense'.

conundrum

A riddle; a question or problem to which there is no obvious answer: 'The fruit-pickers faced a *conundrum* – they could either wear protective clothing and swelter in the heat, or not wear it and be torn to pieces by brambles.'

corroborate

Originally to strengthen in a physical sense – it's related to *robust* and derives ultimately from the Latin for 'oak'. Now almost always used metaphorically, meaning to reinforce a statement, to lend truth to it by agreeing with it: 'His evidence *corroborated* her story that she hadn't left the building after nine o'clock.'

countenance

As a noun, *countenance* is a poetic word for face, particularly a face that indicates character or mood: 'The Knight of the Sorrowful *Countenance*' is Cervantes' description of his hero, Don Quixote; and Shakespeare's

Horatio, recounting his meeting with the ghost of Hamlet's father, says he had 'a *countenance* more in sorrow than in anger'.

Countenance can be used as a verb, too, meaning to support or tolerate: 'I'm not going to *countenance* any interference' is a more impressive way of saying you aren't going to put up with it.

damask
Both a luxurious fabric, originally of silk but later often of linen, and a variety of rose, said to have originated in the city of *Damascus*. Used as an adjective, *damask* is the colour of the rose, a soft pink, and often refers to a woman's delicate complexion. In Shakespeare's *Twelfth Night*, Viola describes a woman who never told the man of her dreams that she loved him:

> *But let concealment, like a worm i' the bud,*
> *Feed on her damask cheek.*

It's the colour of health, beauty and an attractive flush of mild excitement or embarrassment.

delectation
Pleasure, enjoyment, often the kind that makes you lick your lips in anticipation. An old-fashioned word, you could use it in an extravagant way to offer someone something – which could be anything from a musical performance to a chocolate eclair – *for their delectation and delight.*

deleterious

Related to *delete* and derived from the Latin for 'to destroy', this means harmful, either to physical health or to a broader set of circumstances: 'The damp climate had a *deleterious* effect on his asthma' or 'Climate change is proving *deleterious* to the safety of coastal settlements.'

dissimulate

To disguise your real feelings by pretence, to *simulate* something other than the truth: 'I was very hurt but felt obliged to *dissimulate* so as not to cause more trouble.' From the same Latin root as *similar* and *simultaneous*.

doggerel

This was originally comic verse, deliberately written to an irregular rhythm – the word probably derives from *dog*, so perhaps it was the sort of poetry a dog might write. Later, it came to mean verse that was trivial, unoriginal, badly scanned and generally not very good. Perhaps the most famous – or notorious – writer of *doggerel* was the nineteenth-century Scottish poet William McGonagall, who managed to make even the tragedy of the Tay Bridge (which collapsed as a train was crossing it, killing all on-board) sound trite:

Beautiful Railway Bridge of the Silv'ry Tay!
Alas! I am very sorry to say
That ninety lives have been taken away
On the last Sabbath day of 1879,
Which will be remember'd for a very long time.

He's widely cited as the worst poet in history and you can see why.

duplicity

Dishonesty, two-faced behaviour: it's related to *double* and is in a sense the opposite of *simplicity,* in which what you see is what you get. As the nineteenth-century cleric Charles Caleb Colton put it, 'Nothing so completely baffles one who is full of tricks and *duplicity* himself, than straightforward and simple integrity in another.' If you like the sound of this word, it may be worth adding the related adjective *duplicitous* to your repertoire, too.

ebullient

Nothing to do with bulls, but potentially having the same effect as one in a china shop: it means bubbling over, overflowing – either literally or with enthusiasm or some other positive emotion: 'I came out of the meeting in an *ebullient* mood, having persuaded them to fund the project.'

elegiac

Pertaining to an *elegy*, a sorrowful poem, a lament for the dead, originally (according to its Greek roots) sung to the accompaniment of a flute. It isn't only poems and songs that can be *elegiac*: the term can be applied to various kinds of music, moody movies and even to a speech that is especially mournful.

elusive

An adjective describing something that *eludes*, that can't be found or grasped. In Baroness Orczy's 1905 novel *The Scarlet Pimpernel*, about an English secret agent during the French Revolution, the French authorities are famously unable to discover the identity of *that damned, elusive Pimpernel*. But *elusiveness* can also be abstract: a familiar scent might spark *an elusive memory*, one that you can't pin down, or a poet might chase *an elusive rhyme* to help her to finish her poem.

emblazon

Blazon is a term in heraldry meaning the correct, conventional way of portraying heraldic arms; *to emblazon* is to design and colour your coat of arms in this way, or to print the coat of arms on your stationery, the side of your carriage and the like. Not a modest thing to do. In the non-heraldic sense, therefore, a newspaper might *emblazon the news of the celebrity divorce across the front page* or a company might *emblazon its logo* on T-shirts and carrier bags. Splash it about, in other words, with a view to attracting attention.

empathetic

The Greek *pathos* means 'suffering or feeling', so words ending in -*pathy* tend to relate either to diseases or their cure (*homeopathy*, *idiopathy*) or to feelings (*sympathy*, *telepathy*). The prefix *en-* or *em-* generally means within or inside, so *empathy* is entering into someone else's feelings, really understanding them, as opposed to *sympathy*, which is suffering *with* them, alongside them, rather than getting under their skin. *Empathetic* is the adjective: 'You can't be a good counsellor unless you are really *empathetic* with your clients.'

ensconce

To settle firmly and comfortably, usually in the passive form of *to be ensconced* in, for example, an armchair in front of the fire. It comes from an old Dutch word meaning 'a small fortress' but became confused with the French-derived *sconce*. The latter was originally a lantern or candlestick with a screen to protect the flame and is now a wall bracket for holding candles – another feature of a cosy evening at home.

ensemble

This is the everyday French word for 'together' (pronounced approximately 'on-som-bul') and in English means the constituent parts of something considered as a whole. Easier to give examples, perhaps. In the days when a woman wore not only a matching skirt and jacket but a hat and gloves too, her outfit might be described as an *ensemble*; in the arts the *ensemble* is the chorus, the *corps de ballet* or equivalent – everyone except the principals – and *an ensemble piece* is one that they play or dance together, without a soloist. In a film, the members of *an ensemble cast* may all be well known and have substantial roles, rather than there being one obvious star.

entourage

From the French for 'to surround', this is a group of
attendants surrounding a supposedly important person.
It's often used with a slightly sarcastic tone: 'The rock star
travelled with a huge *entourage*, who seemed to do nothing
but ensure that he was supplied with the right brand of
mineral water.'

equable

Even-tempered, tranquil, avoiding extremes: you can have
an equable temperature – neither too hot nor too cold – or
an equable temperament if you are not easily upset. Not to
be confused with *equitable*, which means fair, reasonable,
according to the principles of *equity*. All are from the same
Latin root as *equal*.

exquisite

Excellent, delightful, in a variety of ways. If you have
exquisite taste in clothes, your taste can't be faulted. If
your jewellery is also *exquisite*, it is well designed and
finely crafted. Or you might have *exquisite sensibility* or
feel *exquisite pain* – your feelings are more sensitive or
refined than most people's. Beauty and/or delicacy are the
requirements.

fervent

Very passionate, from the Latin for 'to boil or glow'. So, *a
fervent desire* – whether it's to change the world or to go

out with a certain person – is one that is bubbling over, bursting out of you. You may also *fervently believe* in something (or *be fervently opposed* to it, if you prefer).

flamboyant

Deliberately elaborate and eye-catching, in dress or style: 'He wore a *flamboyant* purple waistcoat' or 'He spoke in a *flamboyant* way, waving his hands and pausing frequently for effect.' From the French for 'flaming' and originally used for a style of architecture that featured wavy, flame-like forms.

flâneur

Someone who strolls about aimlessly, looking in shop windows and allowing himself to be seen and admired; a man who can afford to saunter through the streets because he doesn't have to go to work. What he's indulging in is *flânerie* and if a woman does it she is a *flâneuse*. These are French words, as is *boulevardier*, someone who strolls along *boulevards*, which has the same sense of both fashionableness and idleness. It's very much a 'man-about-town' concept – you can't be a *flâneur* anywhere you have to wear walking boots and run the risk of getting muddy.

galvanize

Almost always in the expression *to galvanize into action* – to encourage or stimulate someone to do something. From an electrical process developed by an eighteenth-century Italian physiologist called Luigi *Galvani* that was used to stimulate muscles. The idea is widely assumed to have inspired the techniques featured in Mary Shelley's *Frankenstein* (written less than thirty years after Galvani had published his findings) to bring the monster to life.

gaudy

Flashy, bright and colourful in a vulgar way: 'I've never seen such *gaudy* jewellery: I know she has lots of money, but she clearly has no taste.' From the Latin for 'to rejoice' and 'joy', which also gives the old-fashioned British term a *gaudy* or a *gaudy night*, a celebration at a school or college.

gesticulate

To wave your arms about in order to express your feelings or make your meaning known: 'I couldn't hear what he was saying, but he was *gesticulating* so wildly that I could tell something was wrong.' Related to *gesture*, *gesticulate* comes from a Latin diminutive, so should really mean *little gestures*, but in fact most *gesticulating* is done on a grand scale.

grandiloquent

The -*loqu*- part of this word comes from the Latin for 'to speak' – it appears in *loquacious*, meaning talkative, and other words to do with speech (see OBLOQUY, for one). *Grandiloquent*, therefore, means talking *grandly* – in an opinionated way and probably using unnecessarily big words.

grizzle

Two words for the price of one, with very different meanings and tones. The more poetic one means to turn grey or grey-haired, usually as a result of age: it's normally used in the adjectival form *grizzled* and is related to *gris*, the French word for 'grey'. Hamlet, on hearing that some friends have seen a ghost that might be his late father, asks, 'His beard was *grizzled*, no?' and one of them replies, 'It was, as I have seen it in his life/A sable silver'd' – in other words, black with streaks of silver. Quite a dignified colour.

Rather less dignified is the *grizzling* that a child will indulge in when cross and looking for attention: a whimpering, fretful sort of crying that goes on and on without getting anywhere. No one is sure where this version of the word comes from, but they wish it would stop.

hanker

To long for or yearn for, often something forbidden: 'After he moved to the country, he found himself *hankering* after the fleshpots of Birmingham.' Of unknown origin, probably Dutch, so perhaps *hankering after the fleshpots of Amsterdam* would be more appropriate.

haphazard

Hap is an old word for luck or chance, related to *happen*. *Hazard* as a synonym for risk or danger comes from the name of an old gambling game played with dice. So *haphazard* was originally a noun meaning a matter of luck, something happening by chance or at random. Nowadays, it more frequently appears as an adjective describing such an event: *a haphazard arrangement of colours in an abstract painting* would mean there was no apparent pattern or order to it.

Also related to happen is *happenstance*, which means chance, or something that happens by chance: 'It was pure *happenstance* that we were in the same place at the same time.' A mixture of *to happen* and a *circumstance*.

heliotrope

Literally meaning turning towards the sun, this is a name given to certain plants that move that way, especially one with pretty little purple flowers. Hence the colour *heliotrope*, variously defined as bluish-violet, pink-purple or lilac-blue. It's a strong colour, as much pink as purple – a purplish magenta if you like – so you can see that it could come in handy if you wanted to describe something of that shade without becoming bogged down in lots of words ending in *-ish*.

horripilation

Gooseflesh, the shivers, making your flesh creep – phrase it however you like, it's a physical reaction to something scary or cold. From the Latin for 'hair standing on end'.

iconoclast

Somebody who attacks and/or destroys established traditions or principles; originally church imagery or *icons*, but now anything that is conventionally deemed worthy of respect. A republican might have *iconoclastic ideas* about the monarchy, while an avant-garde artist takes *an iconoclastic approach* to realistic painting. The destructive act itself is *iconoclasm*.

immaculate

Pure, unstained, free from any form of wrongdoing or any sign of dirt. The Roman Catholic doctrine of the *Immaculate Conception* maintains that the Virgin Mary was conceived without the stain of original sin, which is too complicated to go into here, but adds weight to the idea that she was very pure indeed. *Immaculate* needn't be as high-flown as that, though: you could wear an *immaculate* (or *immaculately clean*) shirt for your first day at the office or have *an immaculate reputation* when it came to conducting business.

impregnable

Not able to be captured or overthrown, originally of a fortress or castle, but also used figuratively: *an impregnable position* could be one that can't be demolished by argument or one where a sports team is so far ahead of the rest of the league that they are bound to become champions. See also BASTION.

impresario

From the Italian for 'one who undertakes', an *impresario* specifically undertakes the production of works of theatre, music and the like: 'He was the *impresario* behind a host of successful musicals.' You can have *impresarios* in the fashion industry and other fields too, but most of them are in the entertainment world.

incontrovertible

That cannot be *controverted*, disputed, overturned – often *an incontrovertible truth* or *fact*: Jane Austen could easily have written 'It is an *incontrovertible* truth that a single man in possession of a good fortune must be in want of a wife' if she hadn't decided that 'It is a truth universally acknowledged' would have a more lasting appeal.

incorrigible

Unable to be *corrected*, describing a quality that is so firmly rooted there is no way of changing it: 'He's an *incorrigible* pessimist: he can find a depressing aspect to anything.'

inculcate

From the Latin for 'to tread upon or trample', this is to instil (information, an idea or something like that) by virtue of constant repetition: 'She's read so many romances that the idea of a happy ending is completely *inculcated* in her mind.'

indefatigable

From the same root as *fatigue*, this means unable to be tired. It's used either of a person – 'She was completely *indefatigable*; I was exhausted but she was as fresh as a daisy' – or of a quality such a person displays – 'Her *indefatigable* cheerfulness drove us all mad.' There's an undercurrent of annoyance with this word: you can't help wishing that the *indefatigable* person *would* get tired every now and again.

inebriant

Likely to make you *inebriated*, intoxicating. This can be both an adjective and a noun meaning the inebriating substance, and it doesn't have to be literal: you could feel *the inebriant effects of the audience's applause* without touching a drop of alcohol.

innocuous

Harmless, unhurtful. *An innocuous remark* is one that shouldn't upset anyone; *an innocuous pastime* is one where no one is likely to get hurt or lured into gambling for high stakes.

insuperable

Not able to be overcome, whether in the sense of a physical obstacle – 'For centuries the Himalayas were an *insuperable* boundary between India and China' – or a desire or feeling – 'She had an *insuperable* urge to empty a bucket of cold water over him.'

intimidate

To make someone feel *timid* – not exactly frightening them, but overawing them and creating a sense of inadequacy: 'She never seems to be angry, but her coolness can be very *intimidating*.'

iridescent

Shining and shimmering, showing shifting changes of colour, displaying the colours of the rainbow, for which *iris* is an old or poetic word. The coloured light you see in soap bubbles is *iridescent,* but you can also use the word in a broader sense – *the iridescent sparkle of the sequins on her dress* or, more fancifully, *the iridescent genius of her ideas.*

irrefutable

Unable to be *refuted*, disproved or denied: *an irrefutable argument*. From the Latin for 'to rebut, to prove wrong'.

irrevocable

Unable to be *revoked* or undone or gone back on: 'The decision is *irrevocable*, so think carefully before you make it.' From the Latin for 'to recall, call back'.

kaleidoscope

An optical instrument, patented in the UK in 1817, consisting of a tube which contains pieces of coloured glass and has reflecting surfaces inside. When you rotate the tube, the glass falls about and is reflected in different ways, producing colourful patterns. The name was created by its inventor, the Scottish scientist Sir David Brewster, and comes from the Greek for 'beautiful form'. Thus, a metaphorical *kaleidoscope* is a profusion of changing and colourful patterns: 'There were so many parrots flying overhead that all we could see was a *kaleidoscope* of reds and yellows.' English words to do with beauty are often spelled *calli-*, as in *calligraphy* (beautiful writing) and *callisthenics* (beautiful or elegant strength), but they come from the same Greek source.

liquefaction

Whenas in silks my Julia goes,
Then, then (methinks) how sweetly flows
That liquefaction of her clothes.

So wrote Robert Herrick in the seventeenth century, in his poem 'Upon Julia's Clothes'. *Liquefaction* means turning into liquid, but this poetic use, describing how silk flows as Julia walks along, takes the word to a whole new level.

litany

In Alexander McCall Smith's *The Saturday Big Tent Wedding Party* (2011), Mma Makutsi is about to scold the feckless Charlie for abandoning a pregnant girlfriend:

'I shall be speaking on behalf of all the women of Botswana who have been let down by men,' she proclaimed. 'On behalf of girls whose boyfriends have pretended that babies have nothing to do with them. On behalf of women whose men go off to bars all the time and leave them at home with the children. On behalf of women whose husbands see other women. On behalf of women whose husbands lie and steal their money and eat all the food and ...'

The author goes on to describe this list as a *litany of wrongs*. It's a word from Christian doctrine, referring to a lengthy series of repeated prayers with fixed responses. When you use it in a non-religious sense, it implies that the list is not only long but tedious: a person who delights in telling you their troubles may be accused of reciting a *litany of woes* and you'd be forgiven for yawning.

lucubration

If you dig back far enough in this word's origins you come to *lux*, the Latin for 'light'; a *lucubration* was originally a work produced by artificial light, the result of burning the midnight oil. This implied dedication, diligence and attention to detail, so it didn't take long for the word to acquire overtones of pedantry and pernicketiness. One nineteenth-century example precedes it with *dusty*, another with *pious* – you get the drift. It's an old-fashioned word and tends today to be used teasingly.

lugubrious

From a Latin word for 'mournful', this is now an almost
comical word for doleful or down in the mouth. Think of
the face of a more than usually sorrowful bloodhound and
you'll get the idea.

luminary

From a Latin word for 'light', this originally referred to the
sun, the moon and other light-giving CELESTIAL bodies;
now it is usually a person who is the 'leading light' in
their field and brings encouragement to others. Often in
the plural: *theatrical luminaries* would be the knights and
dames of the profession.

luminescent

Bringing or emitting light (see LUMINARY). Often used
literally: *the luminescent qualities of the moon on a dark
night, luminescent glow-worms in a cave* or *the luminescent
sparkle of a diamond ring.* Also a favourite of advertisers,
who are inclined to suggest, for example, that their
shampoo will improve the *luminescence* of your hair.

machination

This derives from the same Classical source as *machine*,
but whereas a machine makes something happen or sets
a process in motion, with a *machination* these things and
processes are dishonest, cunning and scheming. Think
Edmund in *King Lear*, Iago in *Othello* or, if you prefer, Ernst

Blofeld in James Bond. All prime examples of *machinators*, planning evil things behind the scenes.

mediocre
From a Latin phrase meaning 'halfway up a mountain' and related to *medium*, this means average, ordinary, in a could-do-better sort of way. *A mediocre play* (or painting or other piece of creative work) isn't bad, exactly, it's just not very original, not very interesting, and leaves you wondering why you bothered to see it.

melange
A slightly pretentious word for a mixture, a hodgepodge of diverse things that don't always come together to form a whole: 'A *melange* of Scandinavian minimalist furniture and fussily embroidered cushions.' From French and pronounced accordingly.

mellifluous
From the Latin for 'flowing with honey', this means sweet, pleasant-sounding, musical and is normally used of words or a voice: 'I could listen to him reading a shopping list in those *mellifluous* tones.'

mendacious

Given to *mendacity* – telling lies. A no-nonsense,
unforgiving word: being economical with the truth is
one thing; spreading *mendacious reports* or *mendacious
rumours* is quite another.

Mephistophelean

Mephistopheles was the devilish character to whom
Faust sold his soul in the medieval German legend and in
various plays and operas based on it; the adjective derived
from his name means fiendish, cunning: 'He devised a
Mephistophelean scheme to get his revenge.' See also
DIABOLICAL.

métier

This is the everyday French word for 'a job or an
occupation'. In English it's a little more than that: not quite
a calling or a vocation, but a cut above something you do
merely for the money. Someone who has *found their métier*
has discovered something that they're good at, that they
enjoy and that, with any luck, they'll be paid to do.

minimal

The Latin *minimus* means 'least or smallest', so *a minimal
amount* of something is a very small quantity: 'He worked
such long hours that he paid *minimal* attention to exercise
and diet.' From this we also get *minimalist*, a term applied
to various aspects of design to suggest that 'less is more'

– using a few simple elements can create great effect: 'The *minimalist* grey-and-white decor was relieved only by a bright orange vase on the table.'

misappropriate

To steal, to take in order to use for a dishonest or *inappropriate* use. The adjective *appropriate* means suitable, fitting, in the right place at the right time: 'However *appropriate* it might have been for her to sing in the shower, it was out of place at a formal dinner table.' The verb *to appropriate* means to take for one's own use, or to put aside for a particular purpose, either legally or illegally: 'We *appropriated* the money we made from the concert to pay for the Christmas party' or 'He *appropriated* the money we made from the concert and left the country.' *Misappropriate* comes firmly down on the illegal side of the discussion. They all come from a Latin word meaning 'to make one's own' and are related to *proper*. See also EMBEZZLE.

miscellany

A mixture, a gathering together of *miscellaneous* things. Often used in a literary sense, to refer to a collection of essays or articles on various subjects and more recently in the bestselling book *Schott's Original Miscellany* (2002), whose contents ranged from military hierarchy to a list of countries where you drive on the left. A miscellany doesn't have to be in book form, however: you could easily find *a miscellany of crockery* in a second-hand shop.

misconstrue

To construe is to analyse the grammatical structure of
something, usually a Greek or Latin text – it's from the
Latin word for 'to pile together, to build up' and is related to
construct. More loosely, it can be to interpret or to deduce:
'Sherlock Holmes could *construe* a man's marital status
from the condition of his hat.' *To misconstrue,* therefore,
is to do this but to get it wrong, to misunderstand or
misinterpret: 'I *misconstrued* his message and didn't realize
what was going on.'

misnomer

A *misnaming*, using an incorrect or unsuitable name: 'To
describe what he was wearing as "a suit" was a complete
misnomer – it was a jacket, trousers and waistcoat that
didn't match at all.'

monastic

Pertaining to *monasteries* and *monks* (and to other similar
religious communities and their members). In a secular
context, sharing their characteristics – reclusive, frugal,
ABSTEMIOUS: 'He lived a *monastic* life in two rooms, never
inviting people in and rarely going out.'

multifarious

Words beginning *multi-* usually mean 'many', as in *multiple*
or *multiply*, *multicoloured* or *multimedia*. *Multifarious*
is having many and varied parts or aspects: 'From the

multifarious sounds of barking, yelping and snuffling, I gathered that the dogs thought it was time for their walk.'

munificent
Generous, bountiful in matters of money. You might make *a munificent donation* to a cause and in so doing would display your own *munificence*. From the Latin for 'making a gift'.

nonpareil
From French and pronounced 'non-pa-rail', this is someone or something unparalleled, without equal: 'He didn't have much conversation, but on the tennis court he was a *nonpareil.*' The English-derived equivalent, less commonly used, is *nonsuch* or *nonesuch,* meaning there is *none such* as him/her, there is no one like them. A palace that Henry VIII built in Surrey, long since destroyed but still with a park named after it, was called Nonsuch because it was the palace to outshine all palaces, of incomparable sumptuousness.

oblique
At an angle, neither vertical nor horizontal, sloping, like this: /. The word has specific meanings in geometry, astronomy and other sciences, but is also used figuratively to mean indirect, not getting to the point: 'He made various *oblique* references to his marriage, but didn't tell me in so many words that he was unhappy.'

obloquy

Anything with *loquy* in it is to do with speech (see
GRANDILOQUENT), and so *obloquy* is speech *against*
someone: slander or verbal abuse, or the notoriety that
this brings to the person being abused. A. N. Wilson's 1984
biography of the writer Hilaire Belloc records that, during
his time as Rector of the Catholic university in Dublin,
Belloc 'attracted the *obloquy* of the Irish hierarchy, who
regarded him … as a dangerous liberal'.

obsequy

Usually in the plural *obsequies*, these are funeral rites, or
simply the funeral. It's often used in a mock-pompous way:
the vicar presided over the obsequies means only that he
conducted the service.

obtrude

If *to intrude* is to thrust yourself inwards, to go in without
being invited, *to obtrude* is to do something similar in
reverse, in an outwards direction: to force yourself – or
perhaps your opinions or feelings – onto someone else.
You might *obtrude your presence* on a gathering where you
weren't welcome or *unpleasant thoughts might obtrude*
when you were trying to get to sleep.

olfactory

Connected with the sense of smell. It tends to be used
either scientifically or jocularly: 'The subtle aroma of

freshly baked bread wafted towards my *olfactory* nerve'
or 'He left *olfactory* reminders of his presence by never
emptying the ashtrays.'

omniscient

Before *Sherlock* came to our screens, not everyone
knew that the great detective had an older and smarter
brother. In Arthur Conan Doyle's 1908 short story 'The
Bruce-Partington Plans', Holmes reveals the depth of
brother Mycroft's abilities to a startled Dr Watson (who
didn't know either): 'All other men are specialists, but his
specialism is *omniscience*.' *Omni-* means all, and *science*
here has the original broader sense of knowledge of
any kind, not just physics, chemistry and the like. To be
omniscient, therefore, is to know everything: in its most
literal sense it is used of God, but can be extended to cover
anyone who *seems* to know everything: *the omniscient
political commentator*, for example, or *the omniscient quiz-
show host.*

orotund

Resonant, booming of voice, or pompous and extravagant
in speech or writing style: 'His *orotund* tones easily carried
to the back of the hall' or 'That *orotund* style doesn't appeal
to me: I always skip over long descriptions.' From the Latin
for 'with a round mouth', and not to be confused with
rotund, which means round all over, plump.

palpable

A *palp* is an appendage near the mouth that some invertebrates have to help them to locate food or feel their way around. So something that is *palpable* can, strictly speaking, be felt or, more loosely, discerned by any of the senses. The word can also have less physical meanings: *a palpable lie* is a very obvious one, while an uncomfortable atmosphere might be *palpable* to someone walking into a room and interrupting an argument.

pander

There's a character in Greek mythology – and in Shakespeare's *Troilus and Cressida* – called *Pandarus*, who acts as a go-between between the two lovers. The noun *pander*, derived from his name, means something a touch nastier than a mere passer-on of messages or arranger of rendezvous; it's a pimp, a procurer of sexual favours who's doing it for the money. *To pander to*, while still not complimentary, isn't as unpleasant as that. It means to indulge someone, to gratify their whims, but not necessarily in a sexual sense: 'He *pandered* to his uncle's vanity by pretending to have read every book the old man had written.'

paroxysm

A fit, a sudden uncontrollable attack, as in *a paroxysm of coughing* or *of laughter*. Also, a climax, the extreme stage of excitement after which things begin to calm down again. The vet-turned-author James Herriot wrote about witnessing a boy's remarkable yawn, describing it as 'a stretching, groaning, voluptuous *paroxysm* which drowned my words and it went on and on till he finally lay back, bleary and exhausted by the effort'.

peerless
Excellent, without *peer*, without equal. You could apply this to the service in a first-class restaurant, the prose of a superb writer or indeed to someone you loved: in Shakespeare's *The Tempest*, Ferdinand admits to Miranda that he has admired many women in the past,

> *but you, O you!*
> *So perfect and so peerless, are created*
> *Of every creature's best.*

She quite likes him, too.

penchant
From French and pronounced roughly 'pon-shon', this is literally 'a leaning', but it's used in English to mean a tendency towards, a liking for something: *a penchant for piano concertos*, perhaps, or *a penchant for wandering the hills in the rain.* A usefully neutral word – there's no criticism implied, but no praise either.

peradventure
If you care to look back at the entry for HAPHAZARD, you'll see that *hap* is an old word for luck or chance, so *perhaps* – with the Latin *per* meaning 'through' or by' – means

through a number of chances; in other words, maybe, possibly. *Peradventure* is formed in the same way and means much the same thing. It's archaic, which means you risk sounding pretentious when you use it, but *peradventure* you won't mind that. Closely related to both is *perchance*, as in the line from Hamlet's 'To be, or not to be' soliloquy, 'To sleep! – *perchance* to dream'. In other words, if he falls asleep he may dream and there, as he goes on to tell us, is the rub.

perforce

Just as PERADVENTURE is 'by adventure', by chance, so *perforce* is by force. It's now generally used in a slightly weaker sense of by necessity, inevitably: 'She wanted me to go, so *perforce* I ended up going.'

pertinacious

Persistent to the point of stubbornness: 'Only a very *pertinacious* interviewer could get a straight answer out of that politician.' The quality this displays is *pertinacity*: 'It took *pertinacity*, but I got there in the end.'

pertinent

Relevant, *pertaining* to the point under discussion: 'The interviewer asked a number of *pertinent* questions about broken election promises.' The opposite is *impertinent*, which now tends to mean cheeky or impudent but originally signified irrelevant or inappropriate: today if you ask *an impertinent question* you are likely to be told, 'That's none of your business', but once the answer would have been, 'Not now.'

pervasive

Spreading quietly, gradually and widely, often in a bad way: 'Racism in politics has long been a *pervasive* problem.' The verb is *to pervade*; it's related to *invade*, with the *per-* meaning throughout. So an *invader* merely goes in uninvited; something that is *pervasive* gets everywhere.

placebo

Literally Latin for 'I shall please', this is the name for a non-drug given to a patient during a drug trial, so as to compare its effect with the substance being trialled. The point is that a patient will often feel better, for psychological reasons, because they've been given *something*, even if it has no therapeutic value: it's called *the placebo effect.* The word can be used more loosely to describe something done to humour someone or to keep them happy: 'The teddy bear was a *placebo* – I wasn't going to give him sweets just before supper, but I had to keep him quiet somehow.'

plenary

Full, complete, often *the plenary session* of a conference, when everyone assembles after attending various smaller meetings. The Roman Catholic Church has a concept of *plenary indulgences* – complete remission of penalties for a repentant sinner – and a person or a committee might have *plenary powers* – absolute, unrestricted powers to carry out a certain task. From the Latin for 'full', which also gives us *plenitude*, meaning a plentiful, abundant, rather joyous sort of fullness: *a plenitude* (or *a plenteous quantity*) *of grass* will keep the cattle well fed; *a plenitude of silk* will make a flowing gown. See also PLENIPOTENTIARY.

precisian

Someone who is *precise* in the observance of religion or of other rules, a purist or stickler: 'It was unlikely that a legal *precisian* and a desperate criminal would ever be close friends.'

pre-emptive

Literally buying before, as in making *a pre-emptive bid* at an auction to get in before anyone else or taking *pre-emptive action* in a war or a negotiation to prevent your opponent from making an effective move. The verb *to pre-empt* is a back-formation (the noun *pre-emption* existed first) and means to act – in order to secure a position, a property or whatever – before anyone else can.

premonition

A feeling that something (usually bad) is going to happen, from the Latin for 'advance warning': 'He had such a strong *premonition* of disaster that he refused to go out in the rain in case he slipped on the wet path.'

pristine

Pure, unsullied, in its original state, from a Latin word meaning 'former or previous'. *A pristine lawn* is one on which no one has played football (or anything else); if you want your money back on a coat you've decided you don't like, you should return it *in pristine condition*.

probity

In one of Alexander McCall Smith's *No. 1 Ladies' Detective Agency* novels, Mr J. L. B. Matekoni is described as having such *probity* that he drove for miles to return money to a client who had overpaid him. From Latin, it means integrity, complete and utter honesty, doing the right thing even when you could get away with the wrong one.

proclivity

If an ACCLIVITY is a slope or incline, a *proclivity* is a more figurative inclination – a tendency or liking. It's often a disapproving word, suggesting that the tendency is towards something shameful: 'He had a *proclivity* for chorus girls in black stockings.'

proletariat

The working class, specifically those who have no assets of value except their labour and are therefore in a perpetual struggle against being exploited by the better off. The word had been around for a while before Karl Marx and Friedrich Engels published their political document *The*

Communist Manifesto (1848), but it gained wider currency in English as a result of their using it. The related adjective *proletarian* is sometimes used in a wider (and more snobbish) context to mean vulgar, unsophisticated: 'There's no point in taking her to the opera – she has the most *proletarian* taste in music.'

propinquity

Nearness. This can be physical closeness, a close blood relationship or a similarity or affinity. There's also the suggestion that the physical closeness may produce the affinity, as P. G. Wodehouse explained in his 1934 novel *Right Ho, Jeeves*. His narrator was hoping that two of his friends would get together as the result of staying in the same country house:

> 'What do you call it when two people of opposite sexes are bunged together in close association in a secluded spot, meeting each other every day and seeing a lot of each other?'
> 'Is "propinquity" the word you wish, sir?'
> 'It is. I stake everything on propinquity, Jeeves.'

prosody

It may look as if it is about *prose*, but *prosody* is actually the study and analysis of verse forms, metre, rhyme, etc., etc. If somebody starts talking about iambic pentameter and an 'abab cdcd' rhyme scheme (both of which, it may come in handy to know, are a feature of Shakespeare's sonnets), you'll know they are interested in prosody. The word's derivation is nothing to do with prose, either – it comes from the Greek for 'a poem set to music' and is related to *ode*.

proviso

The medieval Latin *proviso quod* meant 'it being provided that' and it often appeared as a stipulation or condition in a legal document: you can do *that* as long as you also do *this*. *Proviso* in modern English has the same meaning, but not necessarily within a legal context: 'He said he'd come with the *proviso* that no one would ask him about his exam results.'

puckish

Mischievous, gently trouble-making, like the fairy Puck in Shakespeare's *A Midsummer Night's Dream* (although the concept of an impish character called Puck or Robin Goodfellow pre-dates that play by half a century). It's Shakespeare's Puck who, just for the fun of it, gives Bottom the weaver an ass's head, then makes Titania, Queen of the Fairies, fall in love with this unlikely heart-throb: a typically *puckish* act.

redolent

From a Latin word meaning 'to emit a smell', this is a pleasant term for fragrant or nostalgically suggestive: 'The room was *redolent* with roses' or 'The room was *redolent* with childhood memories.'

redress

This uses *dress* in the sense of to straighten and means to put something right, to make compensation: 'The new president promised to *redress* the people's grievances.' Often in the expression *to redress the balance*: 'Romantic novels had won the competition for three years in a row, so this year we chose a thriller to *redress* the balance.'

repartee

From the French for 'to retort, to answer back', this is either a quick, witty response or a conversation full of them: 'He specialized in *repartee* – he was never at a loss for a smart remark' or 'I understand Spanish well enough if people speak slowly, but I couldn't keep up with their *repartee*.'

repercussion

A *percussion* instrument is one that you strike, like a drum or a xylophone; it comes from the Latin for 'to hit'. A *repercussion* strikes back, in a figurative sense – it's the consequence of an event or action that may continue long after the event itself is over: 'The *repercussions* of the financial crash were still being felt a decade later.'

reprehensible

Deserving to be *reprehended* or scolded; morally wrong, blameworthy. A serious word: you could be removed from public office because of some form of *reprehensible conduct*. But, as with many serious words, you can also use it with a slight shrug of the shoulders: 'I suppose it was *reprehensible* of us to lie about our age, but we couldn't have seen the film otherwise.'

resilient

Able to bounce back to its original position or shape, either in a literal sense or, more commonly, the metaphorical one of being able to recover quickly from a shock, disappointment, illness or the like: you can have *a resilient strain of a crop*, for example, that recovers after it has been attacked by blight, while a person with *a resilient nature* is apparently UNDAUNTED by any difficulties they face.

roseate

Rosy in colour – pink, in other words, or rose-red – or rosy in temperament, optimistic. Used literally it's a poetic word: the nineteenth-century hymn-writer Cecil Frances Alexander wrote of *the roseate hues of early dawn* and many other poets have used it in connection with sunrise and sunset. A *roseate temperament*, on the other hand, like looking at the world through *rose-coloured glasses*, may be just a little bit annoying.

rubicund

Reddish, ruddy, the colour your cheeks might be if you were naturally fresh-faced or had just consumed a sumptuous meal. Although you could also be this colour if you were struggling to control your temper, being *rubicund* is normally a pleasant, jovial thing. The little-used noun *rubicundity* also has a certain cuddly charm.

sacrosanct

Holy. An adjective used to describe something that shouldn't be touched, defiled, changed or interfered with, not necessarily in a religious context: 'My Friday afternoons are *sacrosanct* – I won't book anything except a massage and facial.'

sagacious

Shrewd, penetrating, good at assessing character and discerning motives: 'The mayor was prone to making snap judgements; it was fortunate that he was surrounded by more *sagacious* advisers.'

salacious

Lustful, saucy in a sexual sense, excessively concerned with sex. It's from a Latin word meaning 'fond of leaping', from which you should draw your own conclusions. Often in the expression *salacious gossip*, which means gossip about someone's private life rather than any financial irregularities they may be involved in or speeding fines they are trying to avoid.

scintilla

A tiny amount, a suspicion, soupçon or inkling: 'there wasn't a *scintilla* of evidence, but they were convinced she was guilty'. A *scintilla* was originally a spark, a glittering speck – hence the verb *to scintillate*, to sparkle, particularly in conversation: 'It was a *scintillating* evening; everyone I spoke to was very witty.'

scrumptious

Delicious – absolutely, irresistibly delicious; you lick your lips at the very thought of it. Oddly, it originally meant mean, stingy, and is related to *scrimp* – as in to *scrimp and save* to make ends meet. Somehow, as an American colloquialism, it came to mean smart or stylish, then marvellous and finally delicious. It is usually applied to food but, as with the character Truly Scrumptious in the 1968 film *Chitty Chitty Bang Bang*, it can be used for a person or thing that is particularly appealing.

scrupulous

Having *scruples*, being troubled by doubts about what is morally right and thus meticulous in carrying out tasks or duties. So, you could be *too scrupulous to use office envelopes for personal correspondence* – i.e. too honest to pinch them – or *scrupulous in tidying the stationery cupboard,* in which case it would be in immaculately good order (or even *scrupulously clean*) once you had finished.

sedulous

Constant, persistent, diligent, from a Latin word meaning 'careful': 'She worked *sedulously* to get everything done before the summer break.'

seismic

Related to earthquakes (the study of which is *seismology*, and if you're interested there are lots of other *seismo-* words to do with exploring, measuring and recording the effects of earth tremors). But *seismic* can be used more loosely to mean (metaphorically) earth-shattering, game-changing or just huge: after *an argument of seismic proportions* it's going to take a while to forgive and forget.

serendipity

Always high on any list of favourite words, this is the knack of making pleasant discoveries or having happy accidents. It was coined by the nineteenth-century Gothic novelist and politician Horace Walpole, who claimed to have come across a Persian fairy tale called *The Three Princes of Serendip* in which the princes possessed this gift. In modern life, it would be *serendipitous* if you were browsing on eBay for children's toys and came across something else that took your fancy. But not if you found interesting toys: the point about serendipity is that you aren't actually looking for the pleasing things you find.

sotto voce

Italian for 'under voice' and used, in music and elsewhere, to mean in an undertone. A theatrical aside, for example, might be spoken *sotto voce* – it's intended to be heard by the audience, but not by everyone else on the stage. You can do it offstage, too: 'He told me, *sotto voce*, that his mother was ill, but he didn't want me to spread the news.'

sultry

Of weather, hot and steamy; of a person, suggestive of passion, seductive. Noël Coward, writing in 1931 about mad dogs and Englishmen going out in the midday sun, warned that 'The sun is far too *sultry*/And one must avoid its ultra-violet ray.' As for the seductive angle, a 2015 obituary of the actress Lizabeth Scott, who had achieved fame in the Hollywood films noirs of the 1940s, described her as 'a *sultry* blonde with a come-hither voice cut out for the seething romantic and homicidal passions' of that genre.

surfeit

Shakespeare's King Henry IV talks about men who '*surfeited* with honey and began to loathe the taste of sweetness'; in the opening lines of *Twelfth Night*, the lovelorn Duke Orsino says to his court musicians:

> *If music be the food of love, play on;*
> *Give me excess of it, that, surfeiting,*
> *The appetite may sicken, and so die.*

They are both acknowledging that having a *surfeit* – an excess – of something that is pleasant in moderation can make you sick. Or worse: the real-life King Henry I is believed to have died from eating *a surfeit of lampreys* – a sort of eel – against his doctor's advice. It comes from French and is pronounced 'sir-fit', with the stress on the first syllable.

undaunted

Not put off or discouraged by difficulty, danger or a setback: '*Undaunted* by the bad weather, we walked all the way home.' Related to *daunt*, meaning to intimidate, and pronounced to rhyme with 'haunt' rather than 'aunt'.

unimpeachable

To impeach is to question a person's honesty or integrity or to accuse a public official of committing an offence while in office. *Unimpeachable*, therefore, means unable to be questioned or accused in such a way; entirely and undoubtedly honest: *a woman of unimpeachable character* (or *unimpeachable honesty*). Nothing to do with the peach fruit, it comes from a Latin word meaning 'to entangle'.

unprecedented

Without *precedent*; never having happened before. The noun *precedent* is often used in a legal context to signify a previous occurrence or decision that can justify the current one, but *unprecedented* has broader uses: 'It was so *unprecedented* for them to arrive on time that I was still in the shower when the doorbell rang.'

unprepossessing

Unattractive, creating an unfavourable impression. *To prepossess* was originally to have prior possession of something; from there it came to mean having a prior idea or a prejudice. Hence *prepossessing,* creating a favourable impression, and its more commonly used negative form: 'His appearance was so *unprepossessing* that I instinctively tucked my wallet safely in an inside pocket.'

upshot

The result, the outcome of a course of action, from the name given to the final *shot* in an archery match. An *upshot* can be a good or a bad thing: 'The *upshot* of his advice is that we are friends again' or 'The *upshot* of his interference is that the party has been cancelled.'

veneer

Literally a thin surface of decorative wood applied to the top of a cheaper material to make it look both more handsome and more expensive. Figuratively, a similar concept applied to a person, suggesting that they have good qualities which are, in fact, skin-deep: 'Owning a library gave him a *veneer* of culture, though it would have done him more good if he had read the books.' From German and loosely related to *furnish.*

vertiginous

If you've seen the 1958 Alfred Hitchcock film *Vertigo*, or indeed suffer from that complaint, you'll have a fair idea what this word means. It's often used in the expression *vertiginous heights* – so high that they make you feel dizzy – but you could travel at *a vertiginous speed* (perhaps on a fairground ride that spun round and round) or be baffled by the *vertiginous changes* in the political climate if you happened to be living through a revolution.

vestige

A trace, a slight indication, either literal or figurative and often in the negative: 'There was no *vestige* of his presence – he must have taken away everything he possessed' or 'There isn't a *vestige* of truth in his statement – it's a pack of lies from start to finish.' From the Latin for 'a trace or a footprint' and related to *vestigial*, used to describe the small, non-functioning remnant of an organ such as the human appendix.

voluptuary

A person devoted to sensual pleasure (usually, but not always, sex), or the adjective describing such pleasures. This is a less friendly word than *voluptuous*, to which it is closely related: a woman might have *a voluptuous figure*, while luxurious curtains might boast *voluptuous folds of velvet*, but both of these would be compliments. *A voluptuary*, however, is self-indulgent to an unpleasant degree.

welter

A confused mass or jumble. In early usage the word tended to stand alone: 'It was all a dreadful *welter*', meaning a dreadful mess. Nowadays you are more likely to find a *welter of* something: you might flounder in *a welter of unpaid bills* or, in a violent gangster film, see some poor soul being left in *a welter of blood.*

CHAPTER SIX

Who Knew There Was a Word for It?

Not, perhaps, beautiful on the surface, but intriguing when you penetrate a bit further. Work these into your conversation if you dare.

agelast

A person with no sense of humour, one who never laughs. Pronounced as three syllables (approximately 'adj-i-last') it comes not from 'age' and 'last' but from the Greek *a-*, meaning without or 'non-' (as in *apathy* or *asexual*), and another Greek word meaning 'laughter'. Sad that we need a word for such a thing; good that it should be as rare as it is.

agerasia

The *-ger-* part of this word is related to *geriatric* and is to do with old age; the whole thing means 'not growing old', being well preserved, not showing the signs of ageing. Good that we need a word for such a thing; sad that it should be as rare as it is.

anomie

Lacking social, ethical or moral standards – from the Greek for 'lawlessness': 'Once the revolution calmed down, a state of *anomie* prevailed and looting became commonplace.' You can also spell this *anomy,* but the French form is more usual.

apophasis

From a Greek word meaning 'to speak off', to deny, this is a useful concept in rhetoric, emphasizing what you want to say by denying that you are going to say it. Mark Antony's eulogy in Shakespeare's *Julius Caesar* (the famous 'Friends, Romans, countrymen' speech) is full of it, notably when he pretends to refuse to read Caesar's will:

I must not read it.
It is not meet you know how Caesar loved you.
You are not wood, you are not stones, but men:
And, being men, hearing the will of Caesar,
It will inflame you, it will make you mad.

Of course the crowd does indeed go mad, urging him to read it – which is exactly what Antony wants. You may never find yourself in similar circumstances, but if you do, you'll have the vocabulary to cope.

apricity

A little-known and little-used gem: the *OED* gives only one citation, and that is from a dictionary compiled by a lexicographer called Henry Cockeram and published in 1623. He defined *apricity* as 'the warmness of the sun in winter'; modern lexicographer Susie Dent calls it 'the warmth of the sun on a chilly morning' and either way it's good to have a word for it. You may also like to adopt *to apricate*, which means to bask in the sun.

arctophile

A lover of teddy bears – or indeed of any kind of bear: the Greek origin doesn't specify that it's a teddy. Loving (or collecting) teddy bears is *arctophilia*; if you happened to detest them or be frightened of them, you would be an *arctophobe*, suffering from *arctophobia*.

Lots of words about loving, hating or fearing are formed in the same way: *claustrophobia* is the fear of enclosed spaces, *agoraphobia* the fear of open ones, while a *xenophobe* dislikes anything foreign. Then you can have *triskaidekaphobia*, a fear of the number thirteen; *ailurophilia*, a love of cats; *ophiophobia*, a fear of snakes; *coulrophobia*, a fear of clowns, and so on. Nina Stibbe's 2019 novel *Reasons to be Cheerful* includes the word *ecclesiaphobia* – a fear of the Church or the clergy – which the author almost certainly made up because it allowed her to say something she wanted to say. The point is that, given the suffix and a suitable Latin or Greek opening, you can come up with a word for a love or fear of more or less anything. That might make you a *logophile* – a lover of words. See also BIBLIOPHILE.

bowdlerize

To take out the dirty bits – of a play, novel or the like – usually without worrying about how interesting, dramatic or poetic the remainder is. From the name of Dr Thomas Bowdler who, in the early nineteenth century, published *The Family Shakespeare,* a version of the Bard's works that he thought was more suitable for the women and children of his era than the originals had been. He rewrote, for example, the famous line from *Othello* about 'the beast with two backs', toned down some of Mercutio's bawdy speeches in *Romeo and Juliet* and did his best to remove mentions of rape from *Titus Andronicus* (though with that one he must have found he didn't have much of the play left). Dr Bowdler's name lives on to describe anything that has been unnecessarily 'cleaned up': *a bowdlerized version of his after-dinner jokes.*

charivari

From a Late Latin word meaning 'a headache', here's a term you won't need every day: it's a discordant mock serenade made to newlyweds, created by clattering pans, kettles and the like; hence any discordant din. The once influential satirical magazine *Punch* was subtitled *The London Charivari,* in homage to the Parisian publication *Le Charivari*: both set out to make a noise to humiliate wrongdoers.

Daedalian

Related to *Daedalus*, in Greek mythology the father of Icarus (see ICARIAN), a great inventor and the creator of the labyrinth in Crete. The adjective derived from his name means skilful, but also intricate, maze-like, difficult to find your way through: 'The *Daedalian* intricacy of the wine list terrified him into opting for the house red.' Daedalus' work also gave us *labyrinthine*, another word for unnecessarily puzzling and complicated.

deuteragonist

A *protagonist* is a principal character (in a book, film or whatever), the *prot-* part coming from *proto-*, the Greek for 'original' and -*agonist* from the Greek for 'one who competes or struggles'. Often the protagonist has a friend, a sidekick, a companion who plays a supporting or secondary role, and that is the *deuteragonist* – from the Greek for 'second'. And yes, you are right to be confused, Deuteronomy is indeed the fifth book of the Old Testament, not the second. The name means second law and Deuteronomy is largely about the laws and commandments that God had given to the Israelites. Much of it repeats information (including the Ten Commandments) already given in Exodus which, to add to the confusion, *is* the second book of the Old Testament.

epeolatry

Words ending in *-latry* tend to refer to the excessive love of or enthusiasm for something; probably the most familiar is *idolatry*, worshipping idols or having a great admiration for someone who doesn't deserve it. As with *-philia* and *-phobia* (see ARCTOPHILE), you can make up your own words on this basis – *oenolatry*, which isn't in any dictionary that I've checked, would be an excessive love of wine. *Epeolatry* is particularly appropriate for readers of this book, as it means a worship of words. *Epeos* was one of the Greek words for 'word'; the more familiar *logos* is found in *logophilia,* which also means a love of words, but without the suggestion, implicit in *-latry,* of taking it too far.

factoid

One of the few words whose point of origin we know exactly. The American writer Norman Mailer coined it in his biography of Marilyn Monroe, published in 1973. Well before anyone had thought of social media, he defined *factoids* as 'facts which have no existence before appearing in a magazine or newspaper, creations which are not so much lies as a product to manipulate emotion in the Silent Majority'. In other words, pieces of 'information' that are repeated so often that they become widely believed and create a desired response.

finifugal

The Classical scholar Lionel Tollemache wrote many letters and essays for, among other publications, the *Journal of Education*. It was in this, the oldest educational publication in Britain, that in 1883 he wrote of a *finifugal tendency* which was apparent in both ancient and modern times. He had obviously made this word up: linking the Latin words for 'end' and 'flee', it meant pertaining to or shunning the end (of anything). The late *Times* journalist Philip Howard included it in his 'Lost Words' column some years ago, suggesting that it was 'appropriate for children avoiding bedtime'. Sadly for such a glorious word there's no record of Tollemache, Howard or anyone else ever using it again.

Tollemache seems also to have coined *pandiabolism,* meaning the belief that everything in the world derives from the Devil (as opposed to the better-established *pantheism*, which believes the same thing about God) – and *Anglo-centric,* centring on England and English culture. His *Times* obituary observed that in his writing 'he has some good stories to tell, and he tells them remarkably well ... Thus most of his books have the supreme merit of being very readable.' Clearly a man whose writing – and vocabulary – should be dug out of its forgotten vault.

Icarian

In Greek myth, Icarus was the son of the ever-inventive Daedalus (see DAEDALIAN), whose ambition was to outshine King Minos of Crete. As Minos was all-powerful on Earth, Daedalus set out to conquer the sky. He created a set of wings from feathers held together with wax, attached them to Icarus and taught the boy to fly. Icarus, overexcited, soared too close to the sun, the wax in his wings melted and he plummeted into the sea and drowned. In so doing he gave his name to the *Icarian* Sea, which lies between Greece and Turkey, and to this underused word, which describes overambitious or presumptuous acts that are doomed to end in tears.

kakistocracy

If *caco-* is bad (see CACOPHONY), then *kakisto-* is the worst. Thus, if *democracy* is government by the people and *plutocracy* government by the rich, then *kakistocracy* is government by the worst possible people, those least qualified, most corrupt and generally most undesirable. As with all the words in this chapter, you never know when this might prove useful.

kleptocracy

You may well be familiar with *kleptomania*, a compulsive need to steal, and with words such as *democracy*, which refer to styles of government (see KAKISTOCRACY). Here we have a combination of elements from both those words: a *kleptocrat* is a person in power who happens to be a thief and a *kleptocracy* is a government whose members are concerned first and last with lining their own pockets.

lethologica

In the Classical underworld, drinking the waters of the river *Lethe* made you forget what had happened to you in life. Thus, the prefix *letho-* is connected with forgetting and *lethologica* means forgetting a word, probably one that you know perfectly well but can't call to mind just at this moment. It's a fairly modern term, possibly coined by the Swiss psychoanalyst Carl Jung in the early twentieth century, and it gives a certain gravitas to that embarrassing mid-sentence feeling of suddenly having no idea what you were about to say.

logodaedaly

If you're familiar with the Greek *logos*, meaning 'word' (see ARCTOPHILE), and you know about Daedalus (see DAEDALIAN), you should be able to work out what this rare but wonderful term means – craftiness with words, the verbal equivalent of sleight of hand: 'His *logodaedaly* was impressive, but underneath it all I didn't believe a word he said.' The *OED* online doesn't record a word *logodaedalous*, which would be the associated adjective, but it might have its uses: 'His speech was certainly *logodaedalous*, but it didn't have much substance to it.'

Lucullan

Lucullus was a wealthy Roman general of the first century BC, renowned for the lavish banquets he gave. The adjective derived from his name has come down in history to describe the last word in gastronomic luxury; in the twenty-first century *a truly Lucullan feast* needn't contain thrushes and sweet cherries (as it often did in Lucullus' day), but you shouldn't expect to go out jogging immediately afterwards.

macaronic

'Michelle, ma belle, these are words that go together well'
– as The Beatles wrote in 1965, producing a famous example
of *macaronic* lyrics. In the sixteenth century, it would have
been more usual to mix Latin with the vernacular language
– originally French or Italian – but now you can put any
two languages together and call the result *macaronic*.
Early examples were burlesque, comic verse, not exactly
highbrow, and the word developed from an earlier meaning
that designated anything jumbled or mixed up. Bizarrely,
it is connected with the pasta of the same name: *macaroni*
seems initially to have been more like modern dumplings or
gnocchi, stuffed with all sorts of bits and pieces.

maieutic

Bringing out hidden thoughts, enabling someone to
understand ideas that they have at the back of their
mind. From a method used by Socrates and derived – yes,
really – from the Greek for 'midwife'. Socrates' mother
was a midwife and in trying to introduce his students to
philosophy he likened his role to midwifery rather than
teaching. Pronounced 'may-*you*-tic'.

melisma

From the Greek for 'melody', this is a string of notes sung to
one syllable of text. Imagine a choral work that includes the
word 'gloria' sung as 'glo-o-o-o-o-o-ria' (as in the Christmas
carol 'Ding Dong Merrily on High'), or the way many soul
singers can make the word 'oh' stretch out indefinitely:
that's *melisma*.

opalescent

Formed along the same lines as IRIDESCENT, this means
having the characteristics of an *opal* – a mixture of colours
with a milky quality. The nature writer Jacqueline Bain,
describing the light from a winter sunrise over Scottish
glens, likened it to *a peacock's fanned tail, opalescent and
regal.* So, softer and less shiny than iridescence, but still
lovely.

opsimath

A word that should have become more familiar since the
emergence of the U3A, this is a person who begins studying
late in life. The -*math* part comes from a Greek word
meaning 'to learn' and crops up in *mathematics* (literally
'skill or knowledge related to learning') and *polymath* (a
person who is learned in many subjects); *opsi-* is from the
Greek for 'late'. But clearly, in this instance, never *too* late.

orchidaceous

Resembling an orchid; thus, extravagant, exotic or possessed
of any other quality you care to attribute to an orchid:
'His *orchidaceous* performance distracted attention from
what the rest of the cast were doing' or 'He could have said
FLAMBOYANT, but preferred a more *orchidaceous* word.'

parapraxis

From the Greek meaning something like 'an action similar
to but separate from another one', this is the fancy word

for what most of us would call a Freudian slip: a small mistake or slip of the tongue that reveals a repressed or unconscious thought. Sigmund Freud, after whom the Freudian slip is named, didn't invent either of these terms – he used a German expression that translates as 'faulty action'. The coining of *parapraxis* is credited to his fellow psychoanalyst James Strachey, the man who first translated Freud's *Introductory Lectures on Psycho-Analysis* into English in 1916. Presumably Strachey thought that the concept needed a grandiose Greek name rather than a straightforward English one which people might understand without needing to consult a psychoanalyst.

paraprosdokian

This highfalutin term may sound like something the Ancient Greeks would have used, but seems to have been coined by an anonymous writer in the satirical magazine *Punch* at the end of the nineteenth century. From Greek words meaning 'against expectation', it means a statement that starts normally but veers off in an unexpected direction. An oft-quoted example is the line widely attributed to the comedian Groucho Marx, although he denied he ever said it: 'I've had a perfectly wonderful evening, but this wasn't it.'

petrichor

Words beginning *petr-* or *petro-* are usually associated with rock; *ichor* is the ethereal liquid that flowed like blood through the veins of the Ancient Greek gods. Put the two together, stretch your imagination just a little and you have the pleasant, earthy smell that accompanies the first rain after a period of dryness. You recognize it perfectly well; you perhaps just didn't know it had a name.

philomath

As with OPSIMATH, the -*math* part of this word isn't to do with sums, it's connected with learning generally. And as with ARCTOPHILE and BIBLIOPHILE, *philo-* is to do with loving something. Hence a *philomath* is someone who loves learning.

prelapsarian

Before the Fall; when written with a capital letter, this tends to mean the Fall of Adam and Eve from the state of innocence in which they were created. According to the Old Testament book of Genesis, this occurred when they ate the fruit of the tree of the knowledge of good and evil, which God had forbidden them to do; some Christian doctrines maintain that this is how sin came into the world. Whether or not you choose to believe that, *prelapsarian* is often found in phrases along the lines of *prelapsarian innocence* – that unspoiled, guilt-free condition before we had to worry about serpents, nakedness or what would happen when God found out.

psephologist

A person who studies elections and related issues such as voting trends and statistics. The Ancient Greeks used pebbles or stones to cast their votes, so a *psephologist* is literally one who studies pebbles. The science, if that is the word, of *psephology* is not to be confused with *psephomancy*, which uses its stony element literally: it means divining by studying a set of pebbles marked with special symbols.

purblind

The *pur-* here comes from *pure*, although it's pronounced 'per'. *Purblind* therefore originally meant completely blind; now when it's used literally it means partially blind, visually impaired. But it's more commonly employed figuratively, to mean mentally short-sighted, lacking in discernment or, not to put too fine a point on it, stupid: 'The reforms were delayed by the *purblind* objections of small-minded individuals.'

scaturiginous

Literally abounding in springs – the watery kind – and therefore used (rarely, it has to be said) to mean inventive, abundant, and having a rich and varied vocabulary. The *OED* gives a wonderful citation from a book called *The British Apollo*, dated 1709: 'Thou ... from whose *Scaturiginous* Inventive Faculty, such a Multiplicity of Horisonant Phrases arise', which gives you a fair idea of the tone in which you can use this word. *Horrisonant* – the preferred modern spelling – means horrible-sounding, which again may be just the word you want one day.

sempiternal

A bit of a tautology, this one, but powerful if you want to make a point: *semper* is the Latin for 'always' and *eternal*, of course, means everlasting – so *sempiternal* is everlasting for ever. Really, really everlasting. Some writers have applied it to God and His works, others to things that will always be remembered, but the eighteenth- and nineteenth-century Welsh politician Joseph Jekyll added a less lofty note of despair when he wrote of 'dull dinners ... with the *sempiternal* saddle of mutton'.

sesquipedalian

Coined (in its Latin equivalent) by the Roman poet Horace in the first century BC and a favourite of the more pretentious type of BIBLIOPHILE, this means literally 'of a foot and a half' and can refer (as either a noun or an adjective) to any long and ponderous word or to a person with a tendency to use them: 'Her *sesquipedalian* prose made her works hard to read' or 'As one *sesquipedalian* to another, I confess I love words like "indistinguishability"'.

sybaritic

Sybaris was a Greek colony in southern Italy whose inhabitants were notorious for their luxurious lifestyle. So the name derived from it came to mean devoted to luxury and to sensual pleasures. Sex, shopping or anything in between – a *sybaritic* person (or *sybarite*) will indulge in all of them. There's no emphasis on food and drink, though – for that, try LUCULLAN.

Acknowledgements

Choosing the entries for a book like this messes considerably with your reading and your conversation: you're forever stopping, or interrupting, to make a note. I'm grateful, therefore, to almost everyone I have talked to over the last few months, and particularly to the too-numerous-to-mention friends who have bothered to send me 'good words for your book'.

Thanks also, of course, to everyone at Michael O'Mara Books for wanting me to write it and for producing this handsome volume.

Definitions in the text are adapted from those given in the *Oxford English Dictionary* online (www.oed.com), *Chambers Dictionary*, *Collins English Dictionary* and *Oxford English Reference Dictionary*. The website sentence.yourdictionary.com was also a source of inspiration, but uncredited examples in the text are made up by me. Any errors, snobberies and prejudices are entirely my own.

Index

Words in **bold** are main entries